Teaching the Hearing Impaired
Through Total Communication

Teaching the Hearing Impaired
Through Total Communication

Sheila Lowenbraun

Karen I. Appelman

Judy Lee Callahan

University of Washington

Charles E. Merrill Publishing Company
A Bell & Howell Company
Columbus   Toronto   London   Sydney

Published by
Charles E. Merrill Publishing Company
A Bell and Howell Company
Columbus, Ohio 43216

This book was set in Optima.
The production editor was Susan Herten.
The cover was prepared by Will Chenoweth.

Cover photo by Valerie Brown; text photos by Jan Sm

Library of Congress Catalog Card Number: 79–88499

International Standard Book Number: 0-675-0-8199-8

Printed in the United States of America

1 2 3 4 5 6 7 8 9 10/ 85 84 83 82 81 80

Preface

This book is designed to be used by teachers and prospective teachers of hearing-impaired children as a systematic way of teaching language skills to preschool and elementary age hearing-impaired children. The text has two basic components—one theoretical, one practical. We believe that teachers cannot intelligently plan, adapt, and evaluate their language instruction programs without some background on theoretical and research-based knowledge of normal and deviant language development. We believe, too, that it is impossible to make a rational decision about the use of manual communication in the classroom without an examination of these communication modes from a theoretical and research base. The second section of this book is devoted to developing this conceptual framework.

We believe, as well, that any text about teaching language to hearing-impaired children should be as practical and as immediately applicable as possible. We have read, reacted to, and synthesized a great deal of disparate information; in the latter sections of the book we have put it into what we hope is a format that is immediately usable or adaptable to each teacher's unique educational environment. All the procedures, techniques, charts, graphs, curriculum sequences, and other materials described in these sections have been used by one or more of us in classroom situations over an extended period of time. For us, they worked. We hope that after you have adapted them to your own unique classroom, they will work for you, too.

The necessity for a new book, delineating a new approach toward language instruction for hearing-impaired children, has been apparent for some time. Since the classical works of Fitzgerald (1937), Buell (1954), and Groht (1958), education as a field has progressed; the discipline of psycholinguistics with all its implications for the hearing impaired has emerged; techniques of behavior modification and precision teaching have been applied to the classroom learning process itself; and advances in special education and speech and hearing science have needed to be incorporated into the curriculum and instructional procedures of educating the hearing impaired.

Two themes will run throughout this book. One deals with the impact of Public Law 94-142, the Education for All Handicapped Children Act of 1975. The other deals with the application of Total Communication, the simultaneous use of aural-oral and manual techniques, in teaching hearing-impaired children.

General Problem Area

The challenge of teaching language to a deaf child has been the concern of educators of the hearing-impaired throughout the history of this field (Advisory Committee on the Education of the Deaf, 1964). The primary objective in education of the hearing impaired is successful intervention to meet the receptive and expressive language deficits plaguing this population and limiting their participation in normal communication (Advisory Committee on the Education of the Deaf, 1964; Summary of Progress in Hearing, Language, and Speech Disorders, 1965; Professional Standards for Personnel in the Education of Exceptional Children, 1966). In recent years attention has turned from the traditional classification of hearing loss in terms of pure tone averages (Reichstein & Rosenstein, 1964; Hirsh, 1964) to a more rigorous definition of the implications of hearing impairment for the person's total functioning (Advisory Committee on the Education of the Deaf, 1964; Summary of Progress in Hearing, Language, and Speech Disorders, 1965; Professional Standards for Personnel in the Education of Exceptional Children, 1966). Currently proposed definitions of the hearing handicap emphasize varying communication skills as one gauge of the degree of impairment. (Reichstein & Rosenstein, 1964; Hirsh, 1964).

With this increased awareness of the complex behavior changes produced by hearing deficits, there is increasing interest in the effects of deafness upon the verbal communication. While attention in the field is still partially given to the time honored "oral" versus "manual" (Birch & Stuckles, 1963-1964; Hester, 1964; Scouten, 1964) and "natural" versus "structured" (Hart, 1964; Magner, 1964) language approaches, increased time and effort are spent on the scientific study of the pattern of language acquisition in the deaf child, on grounds that this provides a firmer basis for intervention in the learning process ("Final Technical Report," 1966). The findings of descriptive linguistics, in particular those dealing with the formulation of morphological and syntactic rules, aid in this endeavor ("Professional Standards," 1966).

These findings can aid in the analysis of the productions of deaf children, allowing study of the patterns of communication to show those developmental sequences producing faulty results. Such analysis can also serve as a basis for restructuring the learning-teaching process in order to foster more adequate development of communication skills.

Until recently, most of the studies using linguistics science have been concerned with the secondary communication processes of reading and writing (Cooper, 1965). Although such studies add immeasurably to our knowledge of the communication process, they are complicated by variable skills in reading and are primarily useful in describing the error patterns already present in older children and adults. This limits its usefulness in describing the earliest language productions of the hearing impaired and the emergence of variant syntax at its beginning stages. Earlier studies of expressive oral communication have largely been concerned with categorizing the defects in articulation and phoneme production rather than with the morphological, syntactic, and semantic content of the obtained productions (Calvert, 1964).

More recently, as our knowledge of the complexity of normal language acquisition in infants has developed, attempts have been made to study the emergence of language, in both oral and signed form, in deaf infants. These studies are possible in part because of the sophisticated technology which permits extremely early detection of hearing loss and also because a more accepting society now acknowledges, and sometimes encourages, the use of sign language with very young hearing impaired children.

Education of the hearing impaired is also emerging from a long period of relative isolation from the mainstream of special education. Research endeavors in education of the deaf now are paralleling those in other areas of special education in the use of behavioral technology and objective data collection techniques. This trend does not detract from the uniqueness of the educational needs of deaf children; rather, it enhances our ability to deal realistically and efficiently with the problems presented by this population.

Ten years ago, in a burst of idealism, one of the authors wrote:

> So long as methods of teaching the deaf are based on tradition, rather than empirical evidence of effectiveness; so long as curriculum innovations are undertaken without adequate rationale and lacking a firm experimental basis or adequate control procedures, maximum effectiveness in educational intervention will not be achieved.

Since then, we have learned not to disparage tradition, but rather to incorporate in our traditional methods the fragments of research evidence we have acquired. Maximum effectiveness in educational intervention is a goal to be strived for. Our first chapter is a brief overview of our progress toward that goal through research. In the remainder of the book, we incorporate the educational implications of the available research information with elements reflecting political, social, and educational realities and traditions; from these we present our best guess at curricular interventions.

S.L.
K.I.A.
J.L.C.

Contents

Contents

Teaching the Hearing Impaired

Through Total Communication

PART 1

New Trends in Educating Hearing-Impaired Children

Language and the Deaf

Communication and Language

People communicate with each other in many ways. Essentially, the communication process involves the sending of information over time and space from one individual to another. In human communication, this process can be reversed by alternating sender and receiver roles.

People use different modalities to communicate. Besides the obvious use of language, people communicate orally through laughter, screams, and cries; visually through gesture, posture, and facial expression; and nonverbally through art forms (painting, sculpture, drawing), music, dance, and pantomime.

Most people can use the five senses—taction, gustation, olfaction, vision and audition—for reception of communication, i.e., for acquisition of information from the environment. Taction, gustation, and olfaction are *close* senses. To serve as communication receptors, these senses must be in close physical contact with the communication event. For example, olfaction occurs by the physical contact of olfactory cells with airborne molecules of substances to be smelled, and for gustation to occur the object must be contained within the oral cavity. Thus, for the most part, the close senses bring information about things that are in close physical proximity to the person.

On the other hand, vision and audition are *distance* senses. They allow us contact with the environment without physical proximity. Vision is the most useful sense for perceiving inanimate or immobile objects. It is also the most far-reaching of the distance senses; we can see things that are literally light-years away. Vision permits us to

1

locate the position of an object in space (whether it is in motion or at rest) by determining its relationship to fixed objects or points.

In order to be activated, audition, the second distance sense, requires a voluntary or an involuntary movement by the communicator. In other words, for audition to occur, a sound wave must be generated by something that sets molecules of air or another transmitting medium in motion.

		Reception	Expression
Human language	Auditory	Hearing speech	Speaking
	Visual	Reading print Reading fingerspelling (Reading sign language)	Writing Fingerspelling (Signing)

Non-Linguistic Communication	Auditory	Hearing
		  Cries
		  Laughter
		  Shouts
		  Tone of voice
			Crying
			Laughing
			Shouting
			Tone of voice

	Visual	Seeing
		  Art Forms
		  Music
		  Pantomime
		  Writing style
		  Facial expression
			Creating
			  Art Forms
			  Music
			  Pantomime
			  Writing style
			  Facial expression

FIGURE 1.1
Some human communication alternatives.

Many forms of nonverbal communication are culturally determined. Such things as gestures, postures, and facial expressions have varying significance across cultures. While a smile may communicate approval in the United States, it is considered impolite in some Far Eastern cultures. A burp, considered crude in some cultures, marks appreciation for a meal well cooked in others. To communicate nonverbally with others in the environment requires the cognitive assimilation of accepted meanings intended by the communication. Most forms of nonverbal communication are learned consciously or unconsciously from the environment and play an important role in determining a person's social acceptance.

Until very recently, language has been considered a form of communication unique to humans, having a basic aural-oral form. The definition of language from the mid-1960s might look like this:

1. The structure of language is dual. On one level every natural language has a system of significant sound units (phonemes), and on a second level each language has a system of form units (morphemes) that are meaningful arrangements of the sound units (Hall, Jr., 1964; Hockett, 1958; Miller & Ervin, 1964).

2. Human language is productive. New utterances, which neither the speaker nor the hearer have encountered before, can be understood without difficulty (Eisenson, Auer, & Irwin, 1963; Hockett, 1958; Miller & Ervin, 1964).

3. Human language is arbitrary. There is no systematic or necessary relationship between the features of a language and their referents. (Carroll, 1964; Eisenson et al., 1963; Hall, Jr., 1964).

4. Human language has the characteristic of interchangeability. Any person within the language community can function both as a sender and a receiver of messages (Eisenson et al, 1963; Hocket, 1958).

5. Human language is specialized, "suitable for conveying messages within its own framework of structure and meanings, and having very little direct physical relation to the meanings or acts which it involves" (Hall, Jr., 1964, p. 3.)

6. Human language can be used meaningfully to refer to things or events that are not present and may never have been experienced (Hall, Jr., 1964; Hocket, 1958).

7. Human languages are transmitted to successive generations through learning rather than through physical inheritance.

In the past, linguists tended to agree that all natural languages were primarily aural-oral in nature and, while "for many languages, systems of writing have been devised . . . this does not alter the basically oral-auditory nature of language" (Hall, Jr., 1964, p. 14).

Recently, however, two events occurred that upset some of the notions implicit in the definition above. First, since two *nonhuman* primate species—the chimpanzee and the gorilla—were taught sign language and can now use it to communicate both intra- and inter-species, and since at least one animal taught the language to another, the notion that language is unique to humans has been modified. Second, many linguists have now defined language so that sign language, even though it is not aural-oral in nature, can be considered a natural language.

> Language is defined as knowledge of a code for represent-
> ing ideas about the world through a conventional system
> of arbitrary signals for communication. (Bloom & Lahey,
> 1978, p. 23)

Language Acquisition of Deaf Children

Variables affecting language acquisition

Not all deaf children successfully acquire language facility by the
methods currently used in schools for the deaf. Hart (1964) stated:

> Some of our pupils develop excellent language patterns
> and use language accurately and effectively. Some of our
> pupils use language more effectively than accurately. And
> then, of course, we have our failures, those children who
> simply continue to function nonverbally. (p. 513)

Part of the language teacher's job is to understand and, if possible,
compensate for these individual differences that interfere with the
language-learning process.

In a recent large-scale study of the academic achievement of
hearing-impaired children (Jensema, 1975), the variables of sex, age
of onset of hearing loss, reported cause of hearing loss, degree of
hearing loss, ethnic background, and additional handicapping conditions were analyzed for their effect on academic achievement,
including vocabulary and reading comprehension scores on the 1973
Stanford Achievement Test, Special Edition for Hearing Impaired
Students (SAT-HI). This study made the findings that follow.

Sex.   Females tended to score slightly higher than males in all
areas; however, no significant differences in scores were found
among items tested, except in items testing reading comprehension.

Age of onset of hearing loss.   Jensema divided the population
studied into four groups; age of onset at birth, birth through age 2,
age 3 and over, and unknown. Those whose age of onset was 3 years
or older tended to score much higher than any other group,
probably because their exposure to normal oral language occurred at
the critical language-learning period.

Those whose onset was at birth scored much higher than those
whose onset was between birth and age 2. An explanation of this
apparent contradiction to expected results might be that at least 13%

of the "at birth" group had a genetically caused hearing loss, probably a lower incidence of additional handicapping conditions, a higher mean I.Q., and parents experienced with hearing loss or hearing-impaired themselves (Jensema, 1975, p. 5).

Cause of hearing loss.   Generally, students with genetically based hearing losses had higher academic scores than those with exogenous causes such as prematurity, Rh incompatibility, birth trauma, meningitis, and rubella. This is not surprising, since each exogenous cause is often associated with additional handicapping conditions, such as mental retardation and cerebral palsy, that tend to depress academic scores.

Degree of hearing loss.   The mean achievement score of all subtests, most markedly on the vocabulary subtest, declined in direct proportion to the degree of hearing loss; the greater the loss, the more profound the effect on all areas of language development.

Additional handicapping conditions.   Students with additional handicapping conditions scored considerably lower in all areas than those with no reported additional conditions. Of all handicapping conditions, mental retardation interfered most profoundly with academic achievement.

Ethnic background.   White students scored higher in all achievement areas than black, Hispanic, and other minority group students. However, these data, while accurately reflecting the current situation in schools for the hearing impaired, must be interpreted with caution. Minority group membership is often associated with lower socioeconomic levels, and a lower socioeconomic level tends to depress scores. Moreover, the test used, an adaptation of a test used with normal children, may be culturally unfair and biased toward white middle-class children.

Other variables.   Other extrinsic variables—parental attitudes, age of diagnosis and initiation of parent counseling, restrictions in experience—may enhance or interfere with the language-learning process.

Leading authorities tend to agree that types of parental attitudes are essential to the child's ultimate development (Myklebust, 1950; Harris, 1950; Perier, 1964). They also stress the importance of the child's first teachers—the parents—who promote skills in both receptive and expressive language (Doctor, 1963). Mulholland postulated that parental attitudes are optimal when (a) the parents provide the child with a feeling of security by their acceptance of him and of his handicap; (b) they provide the child with appropriate sex models for identification; and (c) they are not so overprotective that the child cannot achieve his maximum potential (Kirk, 1962).

Since an early diagnosis of hearing loss can lead to the fitting of a hearing aid and the initiation of a language intervention program during the critical language-learning period, the age of diagnosis is enormously important when the course of language growth for the deaf child is determined (Watson, 1961; Pickles, 1957; Huizing, 1960).

A socioeconomic subcategory is created with bilingualism in the home, a variable that presumably affects the acquisition of a language system.

Thus, a multitude of interrelated factors affect the course of language development in a deaf child. For the teacher, each of these variables is difficult to define and varies in its importance for each student. Nevertheless, the teacher must acknowledge the variables' effects, and attempt to individualize classroom instruction.

Language instruction of the deaf child

Because deaf children do not acquire language in a normal fashion, teachers of the deaf attempt to remedy language deficits through formal language instruction.

Miller states: "There are two primary methods of instruction in language for the deaf—one historically known as the grammatical method and the other, the natural method" (1964, p. 335).

Grammatical method. Subsumed under the grammatical method are various distinct techniques that are well known in the field. Perhaps the most widely used technique is the *Fitzgerald Key* (Miller, 1964). This procedure uses Key headings and symbols to classify words according to their grammatical functions. Beginning steps in building the Key are classifications of nouns under the headings *Who* and *What*. Later word and phrase classifications include words under the headings *How Many, What Color, When,* and *Where.* When a sentence is taught, the words of the sentence are written in sequence under their proper headings. Thus the sentence *John saw the dog* would be organized according to the Key headings "Who=What" with the symbol "=" for a verb (Fitzgerald, 1937). Sometimes only one specified sentence form can be written on a single line of the key, since slot positions are fixed in a rigid left-to-right order. Thus, the sentence *John will eat supper later* is easily attainable in the Key; however, the sentence *Later, John will eat supper* can be written in the Key only through a process of spatial maneuvering, producing the written form:

Who:	=	What:	When:
John	will eat	supper.	Later,

The Key attempts to write English grammar at the phrase structure level; that is, it follows a series of rules by which only grammatical sentences can be formulated. However, this grammar is incomplete because morphological rules and many grammatical sentences are not attainable in the Key. Furthermore, the sequence of Key rules presented in formal instruction does not approximate the patterns of language development as it is now known.

The Barry Five Slate System, an earlier grammatical method than the Fitzgerald Key, has been recently used in some elementary grades (Miller, 1964). This system uses six slates or sections of a chalkboard. Five of these are labelled by number's 1 through 5, the sixth is labelled *When*. As a sentence is written on the chalkboard, a different grammatical segment is written on each slate. Thus, the grammatical subject would be on the first slate, the verb on the second, the object of the sentence on the third, the preposition on the fourth, the object of the preposition on the fifth, and the *When* phrase on the sixth (Barry, 1914). An example that fits this grammatical form is:

$$1 \quad 2 \quad 3 \quad 4 \quad 5 \quad 6$$
John ate lunch at home last week.

Natural method. The natural method of language instruction, advocated by such educators as Buell (1954) and Groht (1958), uses what is often termed the "mother's method of language instruction." Language constructions are used extensively in meaningful situations during the school day before they are formally presented in class. The natural method does not prevent structuring of the desired situations and differs from the grammatical method because the structure is in the mind of the teacher, and the child is not consciously aware of its imposition from without (Hart, 1964).

Combining methods. In practice, both the natural and grammatical approaches often coexist, differing in degree rather than in kind. Magner, of the Clarke School for the Deaf, affirmed:

> As soon as a child has adjusted to school life . . . a twofold language approach is utilized . . . One avenue of approach emphasizes an informal or natural pattern of language development. . . . The other avenue of approach is a more formal, analytic one in which basic language patterns are

consistently presented, practiced and learned step by step. (1964, p. 506-507)

Miller, on the other hand, states of the natural method:

> When he is experiencing difficulty, for example, the terms of the Fitzgerald Key may be used or the symbols written above his sentence in order to assist him rather than having him write within the structured situation of the Key. (1964, p. 356)

Each approach attempts to enrich the language experiences of the child by structuring the situation and/or the language patterns to facilitate the language acquisition process. In some state residential schools for the deaf, for example, the Fitzgerald Key is employed in formal language training, while natural oral language is used more often during the school day. Within this traditional educational setting, however, the exact proportion of time spent using each method with a given child cannot be determined.

Traditional studies of the language of deaf children

Cooper and Rosenstein (1966) reviewed early studies of deaf children's language and found that, in common with studies of normal language development, the early investigations of deaf children's language performance were essentially nonlinguistic. Traditional studies were of two general types. The first investigated the performance of deaf and hard-of-hearing children on standardized achievement tests in vocabulary, reading comprehension, or content subject areas and compared it to that of normally hearing children. Research of this type by Pintner and Paterson (1916), Pugh (1946), and Fusfeld (1955) indicates a decided retardation in the written language skills of deaf students in comparison to normally hearing students of similar chronological age or years of schooling. The limitations of such studies are obvious. The samples used in all of these studies were of chronological ages far above those associated with the first steps of language acquisition. Chronological ages of subjects ranged from a minimum of 12 years to adulthood. Thus, the results of the studies, while confirming the presence of language deficiencies in graduates who don't use language correctly, did not provide any indication of the processes used in deaf children's language development.

The second general type of traditional study analyzed language samples written by deaf subjects of varying chronological ages.

Rosenstein and Cooper (1966) maintain that various studies of this type were concerned with investigation of "one or more of the following aspects of deaf children's language: productivity, complexity, flexibility, the distribution of parts of speech, and correctness" (p. 50). They further state, "It must be remembered that these aspects represent relatively intuitive notions and are . . . unrelated to a description of language as a system" (p. 50).

Results of studies by Heider and Heider (1940), Templin (1950), Simmons (1962), Myklebust (1960), and Fusfeld (1955) indicate that the written language of deaf children is, in general, inferior to that of normally hearing children of similar chronological age. Quantitatively, the deaf children studied wrote shorter sentences than their normally hearing peers. Qualitatively, their productions were less complex, less flexible, more stereotyped, more inclined to include fixed repetitive phrases, and less grammatically correct than those of their normally hearing peers.

In two studies that attempted to classify words used into form classes (Simmons, 1962; Myklebust, 1960), a preponderance of nouns and verbs and a relative paucity of pronouns, prepositions, adverbs, adjectives, and conjunctions were noted.

Because of the difficulty in comprehending the oral language productions of deaf children, most of these traditional studies concentrated on written language samples. Since it has not yet been determined whether the written language of deaf children approximates their oral language at any specified age level, information derived from these studies cannot apply to the oral language of deaf children.

Organizing words into form classes, while an easily used descriptive technique, limits research to an analysis of children's language productions on an adult grammar scale. While statistical analysis of sentence length or ordinary measures of sentence complexity provide clues to what the student is not doing, they give little information about the processes the student follows to produce the given utterances.

Legislation and the Hearing Impaired 2

Public Law 94-142, the Education For All Handicapped Children Act of 1975, mandates that all handicapped children between the ages of 6 and 21 and, in most states, handicapped children between the ages of 3 and 5 must receive a free appropriate public education (FAPE). Traditionally, deaf children have received free education; it is unlikely that many unserved deaf children can be found. However, hearing-impaired, multiply handicapped children will undoubtedly be found in institutions for the retarded, and the law is extremely precise in defining the "appropriate" education for a handicapped child. The two major impacts of P.L. 94-142 that this chapter discusses are (a) what the law means by "least restrictive environment;" and (b) what the law means by individualizing education for handicapped children. Of course, neither of these concepts is new; but both have been *mandated* by this legislation.

Impact 1: The Least Restrictive Environment Provision

The concept of least restrictive environment in education achieves its most explicit statement in P.L. 94-142. However, because the concept evolved from earlier legislation and litigation, this section also discusses some background to P.L. 94-142: Section 504 of the Vocational Rehabilitation Act of 1973; rules and regulations of both P.L.

94-142 and Section 504 of the Vocational Rehabilitation Act of 1973; and some relevant judicial decisions.

The laws

P.L. 94-142.　　The goal of P.L. 94-142 is to guarantee equal educational opportunity for all handicapped children. Each state is responsible for developing a comprehensive plan that provides a free and appropriate public education to all its handicapped children. These plans must include provisions for placement decisions based upon the doctrine of the *least restrictive environment* (LRE). P.L. 94-142 requires that the state plans include:

> Procedures to assure that, to the maximum extent appropriate, handicapped children, including children in public or private institutions or other care facilities, are educated with children who are not handicapped, and that special classes, separate schooling, or other removal of handicapped children from the regular educational environment occurs only when the nature or severity of the handicap is such that education in regular classes with the use of supplementary aids and services cannot be achieved satisfactorily. [Sec. 612 (5) (B), of P.L. 94-142]

Therefore, all handicapped children, including hearing-impaired children, are to be educated in as close proximity as possible to nonhandicapped children. This policy is based on the idealistic assumptions that various placement options will actually exist for each handicapped child, and that the nature or severity of the handicap should solely determine the extent to which the child can be educated with his or her nonhandicapped peers.

To provide educational placement in the least restrictive environment certainly does not mandate that every handicapped child be placed in the regular classroom; it does mandate that a continuum of educational environments be established within each service district, so that all handicapped children are appropriately placed.

Education with nonhandicapped children "to the maximum extent appropriate" means that each hearing-impaired child will be placed according to his or her unique needs. The question then becomes, Which educational program is most appropriate for each child's needs? "The least restrictive alternative is the one that realizes the most appropriate match between the characteristics of the pupil and the nature of the educational environment" (Chiba & Semmel, 1977, p. 27).

A popular conceptual schema for implementation of the least restrictive environment is the "Cascade System."

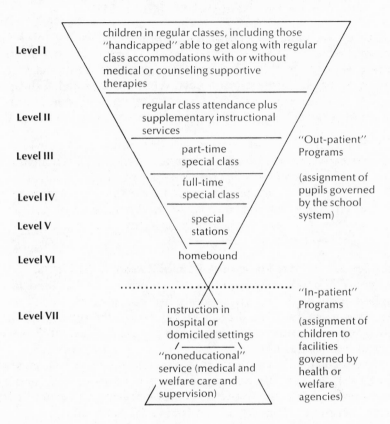

Level I — children in regular classes, including those "handicapped" able to get along with regular class accommodations with or without medical or counseling supportive therapies

Level II — regular class attendance plus supplementary instructional services

Level III — part-time special class

Level IV — full-time special class

Level V — special stations

Level VI — homebound

Level VII — instruction in hospital or domiciled settings

"Out-patient" Programs (assignment of pupils governed by the school system)

"In-patient" Programs (assignment of children to facilities governed by health or welfare agencies)

"noneducational" service (medical and welfare care and supervision)

FIGURE 2.1
The Cascade System.

This system presents nine educational program alternatives beginning with a regular classroom in a regular school, which is the desired setting for the majority of children. Progression through the remaining settings, in which gradually smaller numbers of children are placed, is determined by the increasing severity of children's handicaps and the consequent need for greater amounts of instruc-

> tional and support resources. The most extreme setting in
> the cascade, where the fewest number of children will be
> served, is the hospital. (Abeson, 1976, p. 516)

One of the basic underlying assumptions concerning the education of the handicapped is progress toward normalcy. A handicapped person should be able to move through the educational cascade toward less restrictive environments. Whether or not a handicapped person receives educational programming in only one setting or moves to a more restrictive setting is based on firm evaluative data.

> The crux of the solution is that the planning of delivery
> systems must create one integrated system of alternatives
> open to all children, not one for the so-called normals and
> another for the handicapped. There must be one system
> which is and remains basic for all children and serves as the
> junction for bringing to handicapped children the services
> they need. (Abeson, 1976, p. 520)

Section 504 of the Vocational Rehabilitation Act of 1973. This landmark legislation provides that "no otherwise qualified handicapped individual . . . shall, solely by reason of his handicap, be excluded from the participation in, be denied the benefits of, or be subjected to discrimination under any program or activity receiving federal financial assistance.

"The regulation, which applies to all recipients of federal assistance from HEW, is intended to ensure that their federally assisted programs and activities are operated without discrimination on the basis of handicap" (U.S. Department of HEW, 1977b, p. 22676).

Subpart D of Section 504 concerns preschool, elementary, and secondary education and is very closely coordinated with the provision of P.L. 94-142. A free appropriate education is to be provided to all handicapped children in the most normal setting appropriate. Proper evaluation procedures are to be used to ensure proper placement, and due process procedures are specified to handle disputes over placement.

Elaboration of the LRE concept in rules and regulations

P.L. 94-142. The rules and regulations for implementing the Education for All Handicapped Children Act contain specific references to placement in the least restrictive environment. Part E, Procedural Safeguards (121a.550-121a.556), contains the major rules and regulations concerning LRE. The following is a summary of Part E.

Every state must ensure that each public agency makes provisions for educating handicapped children with nonhandicapped children except when inappropriate because of the nature or severity of the handicap. The provision applies equally to children attending public or private institutions. Public agencies must provide a continuum of special education placement alternatives, including "instruction in regular classes, special classes, special schools, home instruction, and instruction in hospitals and institutions" (U.S. Department of HEW, 1977a., p. 42497). Supplementary services, such as resource rooms and itinerant instruction, must also be available.

The handicapped child's actual placement will be determined at least annually and will be based upon his or her individualized education program. The school the child attends should be as close as possible to home and should be the school the child would attend if he or she were not handicapped.

The child should not only be educated with nonhandicapped peers, but should also participate with them in the nonacademic and extracurricular services and activities of school. These activities include meals, recess periods, athletics, transportation, and health services.

The state must also ensure that all its administrators and teachers are fully informed of their responsibilities for educating children in the least restrictive setting; it must provide technical assistance and training to help them fulfill these responsibilities. The state educational agency must monitor each public agency, making sure all placements are made in compliance with the entire LRE concept and, if necessary, assist in making any corrections in placement.

Other references to providing LRE involve state annual program plans and local educational agency applications. In its annual plan, each state must explain how it will provide education in the least restrictive environment, and state the number of handicapped children participating in regular education programs, as well as the number of handicapped children in separate classes or separate school facilities (121a.132). The local educational agency applications must include assurances for compliance with the LRE provision, and must specify the types of alternative placements and the number of handicapped children in each (121a.227).

Section 504 of the Vocational Rehabilitation Act of 1973. In most important aspects, Section 504 is very similar to P.L. 94-142, especially regarding the LRE provisions. Subpart D specifies that each handicapped person shall be educated with nonhandicapped persons to the maximum extent possible, in order to meet his or her educational

15

needs. The proximity of an alternative placement to the person's home, if such placement is necessary due to the nature or severity of the handicap, must be considered. Nonacademic and extracurricular services and activities with nonhandicapped persons must be provided.

Subpart D also states that if a handicapped child's behavior in a regular classroom is so disruptive that it seriously impairs the learning of other children, the handicapped child's placement may be determined inappropriate. If separate facilities are determined appropriate to the educational needs of a handicapped child, the facilities must compare in quality to those serving nonhandicapped children.

Origins and interpretations of LRE found in jurisprudence

The LRE principle arose from the due process clause of the 14th Ammendment to the U.S. Constitution.

Although many court cases were based on the principle that all children have a right to a free, appropriate public education, the courts also addressed the issue of appropriate education that directly relates to the least restrictive alternative concept.

> Prior to the 1960's, handicapped children were often excluded from the public schools or placed in substandard educational settings without any hearing regarding placement. Consequently, the doctrines of due process and the least restrictive alternative emerged as the legal principles upon which much of the litigation in special education has been based. This litigation in turn has resulted in the incorporation of due process and least restrictive alternative provisions in both state and federal legislation culminating in the enactment of P.L. 94-142. (Chiba & Semmel, 1977, p. 19)

Two court cases specifically related to the requirements of LRE were the *Pennsylvania Association for Retarded Children* v. *Commonwealth of Pennsylvania (PARC,* 1971) and *Mills* v. *Board of Education of the District of Columbia (Mills,* 1972). In the former case, the court ruled:

> It is the Commonwealth's obligation to place each mentally retarded child in a free, public program of education and training appropriate to the child's capacity, within the

context of a presumption that, among the alternative programs of education and training required by statute to be available, placement in a regular public school class is preferable . . . to placement in any other type of program of education. (334 FSupp. at 1260)

The *Mills* case ordered the implementation of due process and least restrictive alternatives not only for mentally retarded children, but also for *all* handicapped children.

In a California class action suit, *Diana* v. *Board of Education,* nine Mexican-American children alleged that they had been inappropriately placed in a class for the mentally retarded on the basis of inaccurate test scores. Among other due process safeguards, this suit led to a provision in the California code that "children of any ethnic, socioeconomic, and cultural group not be placed in classes or special programs for the educable mentally retarded if they can be served in regular classes" (Chiba & Semmel, 1977, p. 20).

In Alabama, the *Wyatt* v. *Stickney* decision concerning Partlow State School, the judge ruled that "no person shall be admitted to the institution unless a prior determination shall have been made that residence in the institution is the least restrictive habilitation setting feasible for that person" (Soskin, 1977, p. 29).

In the case *New York State Association for Retarded Children* v. *Carey,* the court ordered that the Willowbrook State School population of 5700 residents be reduced to 250 or fewer within six years. In a similar Nebraska case, *Horacek* v. *Exon,* the population of Beatrice State School was to be decreased from 1000 to 250 within three years.

Recent attempts have been made within the state courts to mandate placement of mentally retarded persons in less restrictive environments within the community. In Pennsylvania in the *Joyce Z.* case, the judge ruled that a profoundly retarded girl be placed with local foster parents rather than in an institution and that the state pay for the foster home placement. In the case of *Stephanie L.,* in Pennsylvania, the court ruled that a 17-year-old mildly retarded girl no longer required institutionalization, but that she did need a "closely supervised, structured residential program in her own community which could provide essential behavior modification programs to help her adjust to living in the community"(Soskin, 1977, p. 32). The judge ruled that her placement be organized and funded.

Many federal and state court cases have created or upheld the principle of the least restrictive alternative for placement of handicapped individuals. The court cases, together with federal and state laws, culminated in the passage of P.L. 94-142. Undoubtedly, the LRE principle needs to be defended more often in our nation's courts before total implementation can be realized. However, the foundation for insuring this basic right of handicapped children has been laid and will influence future placement decisions.

LRE guidelines

From the preceding analysis of laws, rules and regulations, and jurisprudence concerning LRE, the following general guidelines are deduced; they will be used in our further discussion of the LRE concept.

1. All handicapped children have the right to an education in the least restrictive environment possible.
2. Placement in a less restrictive environment cannot be denied if the option does not exist in a specific service district. If an option does not exist, but is deemed appropriate for a given child, legal precedent exists that mandates the establishment and funding of appropriate placement.
3. A child's placement is determined after the individualized educational plan conference. A child may not be placed only on the basis of a categorical label or a presumed level of functioning.
4. Least restrictive environment is not synonymous with mainstreaming. Rather, it mandates a continuum of services; mainstreaming is merely one service point along that continuum.

Least restrictive environment and the hearing-impaired child

The mandate that all handicapped students be educated in an environment as normal as possible, and that local education agencies be held responsible for the provision of appropriate education and related services for all handicapped children, particularly affects hearing-impaired children.

A hearing impairment that is severe enough to warrant special education is an extremely low-incidence handicap. Small semirural and rural districts may have only four or five hearing-impaired children in residence; they may range in age from 3 to 21 years. For these children who need special education, the choice is often one of placement in a restrictive environment as defined by law—a residential program with limited opportunity for interaction with normal peers, where children are often geographically separated from parents for most of the school year—or placement in a local school classroom. Figure 2.2 shows the range of options available to hearing-impaired children. Everywhere but in the large cities and suburbs, placing the child in the least restrictive environment within the local education agency results in the child's receiving special education in either a one-to-one situation or in a heterogeneous group of hearing-impaired children, where children of varied ages and abilities are taught as one class. Thus, individualized scheduling, programming, and instruction must be done so that each child in the heterogeneous class can receive a unique educational program, designed to help him reach his maximum potential.

Impact II: Individualized Educational Programs

The second major feature of P.L. 94-142 is the mandate that an individualized educational program (IEP) be developed for each handicapped child. This program is to be developed at least annually in a conference of the teacher(s), a representative of the local education agency, the child's parents or guardian, and, if appropriate, the child. The IEP must include:

(a) a statement of annual goals including short-term instructional objectives;

(b) a statement of the specific educational services to be provided to such child, and the extent to which such child will be able to participate in regular educational programs;

(c) the projected date for initiation and anticipated duration of such services; and

(d) appropriate objective criteria and evaluation procedures and schedules for determining on at least an annual basis whether instructional objectives are being met. (P.L. 94-142, Sec. 4 [19])

Individualized instruction for hearing-impaired children

If program individualization due to heterogeneous classrooms and the mandate of P.L. 94-142 is carried to the extreme, many programs exist for each class. In the area of language instruction for the hearing impaired child, these programs within a given classroom might vary on the basis of nine elements.

1. Curriculum.   The content and sequence of the curriculum can be specified for each child.

2. Mode(s) of communication.   The most efficient and effective mode(s) of communication for language input and output can be determined for each child. One child might use total communication input but perform better using only speech as output; a multiply handicapped child might have a physical disability that precludes using speech or sign as output. She may need total communication as input and a language board for sending messages as output.

3. Method of instruction.   One child might learn more through a highly structured approach; another might learn more through a discovery or language experience approach.

4. Amount of practice.   Children differ in the amount and type of drill they need in order to acquire and maintain language concepts and vocabulary. Too little practice and repetition can result in frustration for both the teacher and the student; too much practice and repetition can result in boredom and end the child's motivation.

5. Type and schedule of reinforcement.   For some children, learning language is an intrinsically rewarding activity. They like school and language instruction and need little or no planned reinforcement for continued interest. Others need the teacher's carefully controlled attention and praise to continue working at maximum capacity. Still others need primary reinforcers, such as food or beverage, in order to respond optimally.

6. Length of lesson.   Depending on each child's age and attention span, lesson length can be systematically varied so that the child is involved long enough to ensure his avid return to the next lesson. Within the constraints of classroom practice, however, lesson length is often the hardest element to individualize.

7. Time of day.   All people, including children, have optimal learning times. Some children work harder in the morning; others, just before or after recess. Teachers should realize that the time of day affects children's learning habits, and plan instruction accordingly. For example, scheduling a period of intense academic work early in the school day may be totally inappropriate for children who endure long bus rides. These children may need an opportunity to play actively, and perhaps have a snack, before sitting down again.

8. Type of instructional grouping.   Instructional groups can be one-to-one, small group, or whole class. They can be with hearing peers or autotutorial. All types can benefit from a variety of programmed instructional materials, workbooks, or multimedia presentations.

9. Method of instruction.   Instructional methods can vary, moving from lecture to question and answer to informal conversation; from formal presentation of facts to guided discovery. Different instructional techniques are appropriate for different children. They are appropriate for the same child at different points in the learning process.

Those who advocate the individualized educational program concept regard language development in a different way than do Fitzgerald and Buell. A child is no longer considered part of a group. Her educational program must be planned for her unique needs—needs very different from her classmate's and unlikely to be served using the same instruction at the same time as for other class members.

Group calendar lessons can teach children concepts of weather and past, present, and future time. P.J. is identifying the day of the week.

Evaluating children's progress

Another aspect of the IEP impinges upon the nature of the child's educational experiences. The IEP requires appropriate, objective

21

criteria for evaluative procedures and schedules that determine whether or not the IEP's objectives are met. Since these evaluative procedures are linked to the IEP objectives, they do not involve norm-referenced measures, such as standardized achievement tests. Instead, they involve curriculum-referenced measures, such as pre-and-post-tests or direct, daily measurement procedures used by advocates of precision teaching. In Parts III and IV, each proposed curriculum sequence or instructional procedure is accompanied by the specific objective (as it would be listed in the child's IEP) and by at least one method of objectively recording the child's attainment of the objective. The following illustrates the possible types of data that can be used to fulfill the IEP mandate.

1. Yes/no data are a simple type of data that state whether or not the child performed the activity under consideration. These data are appropriate for such objectives as:

_____ will wear his hearing aid to school daily.

_____ will sign the following 50 vocabulary words.

2. Percent data are appropriate for objectives where some margin of error exists during repeated performances. Percent data represent a ratio of the number of correct responses to the total number of trials. For example, if there were 10 trials and the student got the right answer 8 of the 10 times, the ratio 8:10 or 80% would be used to express performance. Percent data are appropriate for objectives such as:

_____ will corrrectly pronounce the *f* sound in initial position in words 90% of the time.

_____ will add two two-digit numbers with carrying with 90% accuracy.

_____ will discriminate two-syllable words from three-syllable words through audition alone in 9 out of 10 trials.

3. Rate data are used when time becomes a crucial variable in performance. Rate data are expressed in three forms: (a) total rate, or number completed per unit of time; (b) correct rate, or number correctly completed per unit of time; and (c) incorrect rate, or number of errors per unit of time. Rate data are expressed in such terms as: words read per minute, signs per minute, grammatical sentences per day, and subtraction facts per minute. Rate of performance is an important variable when we consider placing a hearing-impaired child in a less restrictive environment. It is important that the child be able to do the same activities as hearing classmates; it is important, too, that he do them as quickly and as accurately as his peers. Rate data are appropriate for such objectives as:

_____ will read aloud from a second-grade reader at a correct rate of 50 words per minute with no more than 5 errors per minute.

_____ will solve subtraction facts at a correct rate of 40 problems per minute.

_____ will fingerspell the alphabet in order with 100% accuracy within 30 seconds. (Rate is the number of letters correctly formed per 30 seconds.)

4. Duration data depict the length of time during which a given activity persists. Duration data are appropriate for such objectives as:

_____ will stay in her seat during the entire math period (45 minutes).

_____ will wear his hearing aid for one hour without complaining.

_____ will not inhale for 10 seconds, while speaking in a normal tone of voice.

Together with the individualized curriculum and instructional procedures, the data collection procedures form the basis of the mandated individualized educational program.

Educational Placement Options for Hearing-Impaired Children

Hearing-impaired children can receive their education in a variety of educational environments. The remainder of this chapter examines nine commonly occurring placement options for hearing-impaired children and explores the decision-making variables that lead to placement of an individual child. Figure 2.2 shows nine placement options currently being used for hearing-impaired children. They range from a totally segregated environment where the hearing-impaired child both studies and lives with hearing-impaired peers exclusively to a totally integrated setting where the child studies with normally hearing peers exclusively, lives in the regular community, and probably has only incidental contact with hearing-impaired peers.

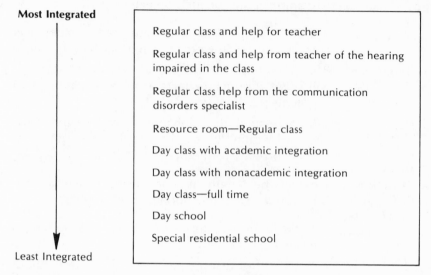

Most Integrated

Regular class and help for teacher

Regular class and help from teacher of the hearing impaired in the class

Regular class help from the communication disorders specialist

Resource room—Regular class

Day class with academic integration

Day class with nonacademic integration

Day class—full time

Day school

Special residential school

Least Integrated

FIGURE 2.2
Nine placement options for hearing-impaired children.

Residential schools

The special residential school for the hearing impaired has been a mainstay of the educational service system since 1817 when Thomas Gallaudet and Laurent Clerc returned from France to establish the American Asylum for the Education of the Deaf and Dumb. This school, now called the American School for the Deaf, currently enrolls 383 deaf pupils (American Annals of the Deaf, April 1978).

A residential school for the hearing impaired can be defined as a school program, operated by either a government agency or a private corporation, where at least some of the students are accommodated on campus in dormitories or cottages while they attend the program. Many residential schools have a substantial number of day students who are bussed in daily from the surrounding community. Many schools also have a 5-day residential option for those students who live near enough to go home every weekend. For some students, however, attending a residential school still means isolation from their hearing peers, community, and families for prolonged periods; it means going home only on major holidays (Thanksgiving, Christmas, and Easter) and over the summer vacation.

If the least restrictive environment provision of Public Law 94-142 is taken to mean provision of maximum opportunity for interaction with normally hearing peers and instruction in an educational environment as close to normal as possible, then the residential school surely is the most restrictive environment where hearing-impaired children can be educated. On the other hand, residential schools usually have a large enough population to have homogeneous classes with children of similar age/ability level grouped together. They also are likely to have the population base for providing a full range of course offerings, such as vocational classes and academic electives, especially at the high school level. Generally, residential schools provide a large selection of extracurricular activities such as team sports, hobby clubs, Boy and Girl Scout troops, and religious education; all these activities are specifically designed and appropriate for hearing-impaired children.

Language instruction in residential programs will differ in content to some degree from instruction in day programs. Because children live for the most part in dormitories or cottages where they do not experience normal family activities, the language for such activities as cooking meals, doing dishes, cleaning the house, washing clothes, and shopping at the supermarket must be formally taught in school if it is to be learned. If the child resides apart from his family for weeks or months at a time, a real communication gap can easily develop between parents and child. The parents' lack of skills in total communication and their lack of close involvement with the child's day-to-day school experiences are likely to impede language instruction or even social interaction in the home. On the positive side, at a residential school where total communication is used consistently by teachers, other staff members, and the hearing-impaired students, a child is likely to acquire a lot of incidental language from watching people converse around him.

Day schools

Day schools, too, have a place in the history of education of the hearing impaired in the United States. The first day school, the Boston School for the Deaf, now renamed the Horace Mann School for the Deaf in Boston, was established in 1869 and is still in existence today.

Day schools are defined as schools run by a local education agency (LEA), jointly by several LEA's, or privately. Day school enrollment may be limited to hearing-impaired children. These schools are administratively and usually geographically separate from regular elementary and secondary schools, and tend to exist only in large urban or suburban areas where a sufficient number of hearing-impaired children live within bussing range to warrant a separate school establishment.

Day schools are similar to residential schools because both academic instruction and nonacademic activities are carried out in a segregated educational environment. Generally, classes are homogeneous by age/ability level. Day schools differ from residential schools because students return home each day. Thus, there are potential opportunities for integration into the community, interaction with normally hearing peers, and full participation in family life. However, the range of extracurricular activities geared to the hearing-impaired child, and the possibilities of incidental language learning through watching the conversations of other people using total communication in non-school settings are often sharply reduced.

Day classes

Day classes for the deaf comprise the next three options for placement of a hearing-impaired child. Day classes are defined as one or more special classes for the hearing impaired located in or adjacent to a school for normally hearing children of similar age. A day-class program can range from one class of heterogeneously grouped hearing-impaired children (perhaps aged 5 through 12) located in a regular elementary school, to a program with 15 or 20 classes located sequentially in a regular elementary school, junior high school, and high school. Once classes for the hearing impaired are located near classes for normally hearing children and administratively linked to such classes, the degree of interaction with hearing peers can be tailored to the needs and abilities of each hearing-impaired student.

Day-class options.   One option is to place hearing-impaired children in a special day class, without facilitating any integration or interaction with hearing peers, other than through casual contact in corridors and play areas. In smaller programs, where only one or two heterogeneous classes of hearing-impaired children exist, a child may have the same teacher for several years (perhaps as many as five or six) and interact with essentially the same limited peer group. These groups sometimes become as close-knit as families, developing their own customs, traditions, and even a language system. An esoteric, nonverbal gesture system often develops that is clearly understood by each member of the small group but not by outsiders, including other deaf peers and adults. Such a system makes it extremely difficult for the children to pursue their education in classes for normally hearing students, or in other special classes for the deaf.

A second day class placement option is to provide structured opportunities for integration in nonacademic areas of study such as physical, vocational, and art education classes. In this option, the hearing-impaired student continues to receive all academic education in a segregated class. The curriculum offered is not necessarily the same as that offered to hearing children of similar age/ability levels, although parallel curricula offers the maximum opportunity for future integration.

The third day-class placement option is to provide the hearing-impaired student with structured opportunity for integration during one or more academic periods. While the child receives most academic instruction for one or more subjects in the special classroom, she is placed in a regular class with normally hearing peers of similar age/ability levels for other subjects, generally math, science, or social studies. In this and other integration situations, the services of an interpreter or interpreter/tutor is nearly always essential. The interpreter accompanies the child to class and assures the child access to the communication system used in the classroom. In addition, for junior and senior high school classes, as well as for postsecondary classes, notetakers should be provided because a hearing-impaired person has difficulty following a lecture visually (using sign language or speechreading), taking notes at the same time. In all situations where an interpreter is employed, both the instructor and the student should be informed of the rules and procedures governing this service. (See p. 29)

In all the day-class options, the administrative, teaching, and evaluative responsibilities are in the hands of the special education program; the regular education program plays a supportive role. However, the following four options show a shift in primary responsibilities from special education programs to regular education programs. The shift indicates that the instructional decision making, including decisions about curriculum, is primarily in the hands of the regular teachers and administrators, while teachers of the hearing impaired and other support personnel involved are in an advisory capacity.

Resource room option.   The resource room placement option allows a qualified hearing-impaired child to receive the majority of his academic and nonacademic instruction with his normally hearing classmates. However, for fixed periods daily, the child leaves the classroom for instruction by a teacher of the hearing impaired. Special instruction is usually given in areas of language, speech, auditory training, and/or reading. It is essential that the resource room teacher and the homeroom teacher be in close contact so that activities in the resource room will complement those in the regular classroom. Again, the child may be afforded the service of an interpreter or interpretor/tutor while in the regular class.

Integration with support services.   In the next three options, the child remains in the regular classroom for all academic subjects, but receives special help in a variety of ways.

The child can stay full time in the regular class but receive help from communication disorders specialists and/or educational audiologists in speech, language development, and/or auditory training.

The child could also stay in the regular classroom but receive ancillary services in the classroom from a teacher of the hearing impaired, a tutor, a specially trained teacher's aide, or an interpreter-tutor. Here, the service provider works under the instructional supervision of the regular teacher and tutors those subject areas covered in regular class. The service provider's role is very different from that of the resource room teacher, who covers material complementary to, but not necessarily identical with, the regular curriculum.

A final option allows the child to remain full time in a regular classroom, using the services of an interpreter if necessary, but receiving no other direct instructional support. The child's teacher may need help to modify curriculum and instruction for the hearing-impaired child. Such help would be provided by a consultant teacher of the hearing impaired.

Whenever a hearing-impaired child receives all or part of her education in a regular classroom, every effort must be made to ensure that, while providing the least restrictive environment possible, the quality of her education is not diminished. While it is legally and morally wrong to segregate a handicapped child on the basis of his handicap alone, it is just as wrong to place him in an integrated environment where he is not emotionally, socially, or academically able to cope. Both the child and the environment must be carefully prepared for integration.

Guidelines for integrating hearing-impaired children

The following are offered as guidelines to the integration of hearing-impaired children in normal classrooms.

1. Each classroom used for hearing-impaired children should be sound-treated in consultation with an audiologist.
2. Each child considered for placement in a regular class should have her hearing ability evaluated in the classroom or other area (e.g., art room, gym) where she will work. The hearing aid she wears should have the most suitable amplication characteristics.

Teachers and administrators who deal with the hearing-impaired child should have access to inservice training in the following areas.

1. The nature of hearing-impaired children.
2. The functional hearing ability of the students in their classes
3. Methods of facilitating lipreading in the regular classroom
4. Language development of hearing-impaired children
5. The form of manual communication (if any) used by the child
6. Methods of working productively as a team member to ensure the most appropriate education for the hearing-impaired child

If the child is aided by an interpreter or interpreter/tutor, the child, the teacher, and the interpreter must agree beforehand on an explicit code of behavior for all concerned. This agreement should cover such items as: (a) the amount of help, other than straight translation, the interpreter gives the child; (b) the degree to which the interpreter converts the childs' utterances into straight language; (c) circumstances in which the child does not use an interpreter; (d) the degree to which the teacher addresses the interpreter directly with questions such as "Do you think he understood that?" and (e) special lighting and seating requirements, including the flexibility for both the interpreter and the child to change seats for different classroom activities.

Hearing peers also need to be specifically instructed on the nature of hearing impairment and on such special concerns as "Why she can't talk right."

PART 2

Instructional Procedures in Language Teaching

Systematic Instruction

Educational research indicates that children learn best (most quickly and most efficiently) when they are taught the precise skills that they are supposed to acquire. This method is more effective than teaching children indirectly or giving them broad experiences where skills are first deduced and then learned. The rest of this text shows teachers how to provide systematic language instruction to hearing-impaired children. A systematic instructional model allows the teacher to go through an invariant series of steps in order to teach each behavioral objective assigned to each child. These steps allow the teacher to make rational, data-based decisions and account for the results of his decision-making process.

The systematic instructional model is presented in Figure 3.1, p. 40. Each of the six components of the model will be defined and discussed in this chapter.

Component 1: Perform Initial Assessment

To adequately plan a program for a child, the teacher must determine where the child is currently functioning in the specific subject area to be taught. The assessment used is important because the more specific the assessment, the more precise the teacher's ability to place the child, and the more precise his placement in the curriculum. Several different types of tests are used with hearing-impaired children. On entering your class, the child will probably have taken current audiological exams and intelligence tests; if the child is above preschool age, he has taken achievement tests. You can use results of these tests to predict the rate at which the child can move through the curriculum, as well as to predict the communication modalities he is likely to use. Intelligence tests and achievement tests are both norm-referenced; that is, they compare the child's performance on the test with the test performance of other children of similar chronological age. Thus, the test results tell you how well the hearing-impaired child is doing in comparison to his normally hearing peers. This information is essential when mainstreaming is considered. Other tests tell how well the hearing- impaired child is doing by comparing her to a normative group of hearing-impaired children. These tests may give you a rough indication of where to start in a curriculum sequence, but they do not indicate precise areas where he is proficient or deficient.

To be maximally useful to you in pinpointing the place to begin instruction, a test must be curriculum-referenced and criterion-referenced. That is, the test should be based on the curriculum materials the child is expected to learn and have a specified criterion for either passing or failing an item on the test. The test should also be constructed so that you can analyze errors, determining whether or not they fall into any recognizable pattern. A good example of a traditionally used curriculum-referenced test is the articulation test, because one curriculum goal for most hearing-impaired children is that they say all English language phonemes in an intelligible fashion. Thus, commercial tests have been devised that require children to attempt the articulation of each phoneme (usually in words in initial medial and final position). An analysis of test results will indicate the precise sounds that the child cannot articulate properly and, therefore, the entering point for that portion of the speech curriculum. Further analysis of the incorrect responses may show a pattern of errors that is amenable to specific training. For example, the child may substitute voiced for voiceless stops or may introduce nasality into all back vowels. This type of information can be used to formulate specific educational objectives and employ specific strategies to ameliorate the error patterns.

Therefore, to be maximally useful to you, an initial assessment must:

1. precede the introduction of any new curriculum unit;
2. be specific regarding the skills and knowledge to be acquired in that unit;
3. permit direct analysis of error responses; and

4. yield results that are translatable into educational objectives and the use of specific strategies.

Part IV of this book will present examples of specific assessment instruments that are used in conjunction with vocabulary and syntax units.

Component 2: Establish Long- and Short-Term Objectives

Based on the initial assessment results and your knowledge of both the curriculum and the child's probable rate of progress, you will write objectives for each child. A long-term objective states where you expect the child to be by the end of the school year or another reporting period. Short-term objectives state the intermediate steps the child must take in order to reach the long-term objectives. Both are written in behavioral terms.

These objectives become part of the child's individualized educational program and state, in measurable terms, the child's expected progress through the curriculum. Each behavioral objective has five components.

1. *Who* The child's name or the group name is given.

2. *Will do what* The specific task is stated in measurable, observable terms. Verbs such as *read* (words), *say* (words), *sign* (sentences), *fingerspell* (words), *jump, solve* (problems) can be observed. Verbs such as *know, understand, comprehend,* and *realize* are not appropriate because you cannot measure *knowing* unless the products of knowledge through speech, sign or writing are observed.

3. *Under what conditions* Also stated are the specific materials and aids to be used and the conditions that will prove the objectives' fulfillment. The directions used to elicit the proper response are often included in this statement, e.g., *when asked by the teacher* or *given a ruler and a compass.*

4. *To what criterion* The measurement to be used is another component of the behavioral objective. The measurement determines when the student meets the objective and is ready for the next phase of the curriculum. Such terms as *100% of the time, always, never, with 90% accuracy, at a rate of 50 words per minute* are used. These specific words dictate to you the data recording system you must maintain.

5. *By what date*   Finally, the behavioral objective includes the best guess of the time the student will take to master the objective according to the criterion. Although these guesses are not binding, they should be good approximations based on your knowledge of the complexity of the task involved and your previous experience with the student.

In summary, the entire behavioral objective uses this format: *Who, will do what, under what conditions, to what criterion, by what date.*

Component 3: Select Instructional Activities

After formulating the long- and short-term objectives based on assessment data and on the curriculum areas to be covered, you must plan specific tasks that help the child achieve the stated objectives. Planning tasks is perhaps the most critical and least understood part of the systematic instructional process. It requires you to recognize many diverse elements and mold them into a unified educational plan. Some of these elements are discussed in the following paragraphs.

Dictates of the objectives

The instructional activities selected must be appropriate for the type of objective written. Four basic learning objectives, corresponding to the four stages of learning, affect your educational plan.

Initial acquisition.   The child learns to do something he has never done before, for example, he pronounces the /k/ phoneme in isolation for the first time and does it again enough times that you determine that he can now voluntarily produce that sound.

Fluency.   After the child has learned a new task, she must have sufficient opportunity to practice it so that the new knowledge or skill becomes a permanent part of her repertoire. Generally, this phase requires varying types of drill activities.

Generalization.   Because the new knowledge or skill is not fully habitual in the original learning situation, it is applied to all appropriate situations. Using our example of the /k/ phoneme in this phase, we expect that the child will have gained some degree of fluency in the use of /k/ in the tutoring situation, and can now use the sound during all classroom activities. If possible, this program should be followed at home, too.

Maintenance.   Any skill or knowledge that is acquired must be used or reviewed periodically so that it is not lost. At times, prior skill or knowledge is used automatically when more complex problems are presented. For example, simple subtraction facts are automatically practiced when multiplication and division of large numbers are learned. In other areas however, such as the learning of new seasonal vocabulary words, the opportunities for automatic practice are more limited. Christmas words such as *Santa Claus* and *candy cane* or a Halloween word like *jack-o-lantern* do not usually come up in classroom work during the January through June season. For hearing-impaired children these must be maintained in the child's repertoire of knowledge through regular review.

Dictates of time, space, and personnel

Each teacher must be accountable for making the best possible use of the time, space, and personnel alloted to him for educating the children in the class. Both the instructional needs of each child and the instructional needs of the group must be balanced. For example, whenever one child is given one-to-one instruction, the rest of the group is not receiving individual instruction but is taught as a group or asked to work independently. For each classroom, the teacher must set out a balanced instructional program for large group, small group, individual, and independent activities. He is in charge of allocating the instructional tasks most effectively among himself, classroom aides, and volunteers; he must also schedule the use of available space and time.

Consideration of the available materials

The instructional activities selected depend somewhat on the availability of materials necessary to implement them. Materials can either be commercially prepared or teacher-made. Various types of materials are available, including (a) visual materials: movies, slides, pictures, TV programs, or videotapes; (b) auditory materials: tapes or records; (c) printed materials: books, newspapers, magazines, flashcards, or duplicated sheets; and (d) programed instruction, or computer assisted instruction. Each available material should be examined for its relevance to the stated objectives. Some may be suitable for immediate use, while others may have to be adapted or supplemented with teacher-made components. Frequently, suitable materials cannot be found and the teacher must create the needed instructional components. The search for useful materials is greatly facilitated when the teacher has access to an information and materials retrieval system, such as ERIC. In addition, teachers should maintain a filing system for teacher-made materials so that they can retrieve the materials easily and use them again.

Consideration of learner needs

In addition to all the considerations mentioned so far, you must plan instructional activities suited to each child, according to his strengths and weaknesses. Such factors as the child's preferred modes of communication, and his auditory ability, cognitive ability (which dictates the size of the instructional tasks to be programmed), and emotional needs must be considered while planning activities. These factors dictate the nature and schedule of reinforcement to be used, the length of the instructional period, and the setting for instruction.

Component 4: Select Data Recording Systems

Part I discussed the possible types of data to be collected. On the basis of the behavioral objectives written and the instructional activities selected, you must now determine the specific system you will use for recording data. This involves creating the charts and graphs for recording the data, determining the frequency of data collection, and selecting the precise instructional event during which data will be collected.

For example, suppose the instructional objective specifies that Beth will *say* and *sign* a list of 10 particular vocabulary words with 100% accuracy when she is shown pictures of the appropriate objects. The data form dictated by the objective is percent data. The instructional event to be monitored is the presentation of appropriate pictures for which Beth will say and sign the vocabulary words. Note that presenting pictures is not necessarily the only instructional activity used to *teach* the words. Other activities might involve creative dramatics, movies, language-experience stories, and many more experiences using the target words. Periodically, however, the 10 pictures will be presented and the percent of Beth's correct responses will be noted on an appropriate chart or graph. When she reaches the 100% criterion, another more difficult instructional objective can be introduced.

Component 5: Implement Instructional Plan

Only after carefully carrying out the first four components can you begin actual instruction. During instruction, the teacher evaluates

Individual reading instruction is used effectively with Greg in a daily tutoring session.

progress to ensure that the child is learning near or above the desired rate. If the child is progressing well, the instruction continues until he meets the objective. If he is not progressing well, the instructional activities, materials, or perhaps even the objectives themselves need revision.

Component 6: Modify Instructional Plan

On the basis of data obtained from the instructional procedures, you must now decide where to go next with the child. If she behaved as you predicted, she met the stated objective and can once again be assessed before beginning to work on the next objective in the curriculum. If her performance was better than expected, the time-line could be decreased, or the amount of material to be mastered in the next instructional sequence could be increased. If she performed more poorly than anticipated, the next short-range objectives and/or the instructional activities should be reevaluated so that she can progress faster through the next sequence. The exact cause of the problem will become apparent when you analyze the data obtained, carefully observing the pattern of incorrect responses.

Using a systematic instructional model, a teacher gets information on the current status of the child in the area to be taught. The results of this initial assessment are used in formulating precise learning objectives for the child. The teacher then searches for those instructional activities that are most likely to lead to the child's mastery of the objectives. She formulates a plan for obtaining the data about the child's progress toward the objectives. Only after this does the instruction actually take place, with the teacher being ready to modify her instructional procedure in response to the data obtained.

In a systematic educational model, the teacher uses his own expert knowledge of the child, the curriculum, and the materials available. Guided by precise data, he makes rational decisions that permit the child to progress as rapidly as possible through the learning process.

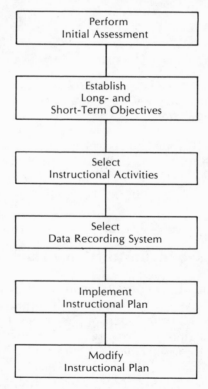

FIGURE 3.1
A systematic instructional model

Total Communication and Specific Instructional Techniques

The Importance of Saying and Signing Complete English Sentences

The practical use of total communication involves saying and signing words simultaneously. The most effective learning occurs when both teacher and child say and sign every word in every sentence. Two major benefits resulting from this technique are:

1. Through consistent exposure to complete English sentences, hearing-impaired children become accustomed to them as the normal means of communication. In this way, children develop expectations of seeing and receiving complete English.

2. Children learn that they, too, must produce complete English sentences because the teacher expects them to say and sign complete sentences. Correct English is praised, whether it be independently produced or cued by the teacher. If attempts at complete sentences are the acceptable means of communication in the classroom, children will develop the habit of using them. And, as a result, correct English will be regarded as normal and valuable.

Teacher-to-child communication

A skillful teacher will take the time to say and sign each word when communicating with hearing-impaired children. The teacher should communicate slowly and clearly, while maintaining the rhythm of connected speech. In this way, all elements of the sentence are distinct to the child; each component of a sentence should be distinguishable as a separate entity for optimum learning to occur. When English is spoken and signed slowly and completely, the teacher avoids the possibility of the child's receiving partial sentence patterns or a series of syllables run together.

Total communication, used in this way, is also appropriate for an oral child. The oral child still needs to observe and receive complete sentence patterns for optimum English learning. This total communication input can have direct benefits for oral-only output.

Child-to-teacher communication

The teacher can positively influence the type of total communication habits the child develops by her requirements for child output.

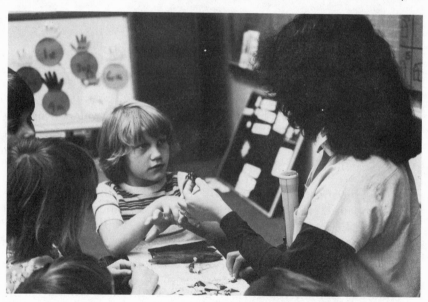

The language experience approach combines interesting activities with specific objectives. The classroom teacher is showing Susan the correct sign for crab.

The following important habits can be developed and expected by the teacher:

1. consistent attempts at accurate signing as part of total communication skills;
2. consistent attempts at precise speech as part of total communication skills; and
3. consistent attempts to communicate in English sentences.

These habits can be established by a teacher who:

1. models correct behavior by clearly saying and signing complete English sentences;
2. lets the child know careless output is unacceptable by cueing and then expecting a correct production; and
3. enthusiastically praises precise communications, letting the child know such habits are highly valued.

Generally, hearing-impaired children should be required to say and sign every word, not only for the development of English, but also for the development of clear speech. For oral children, speech, unaccompanied by signs, is the optimum mode of communication. Occasionally, a child with enough functional residual hearing to have precise speech has difficulty coordinating signs with his speech, resulting in stilted communication. Determining this to be the case with a particular child, the teacher may decide to expect only oral output from the child. Teacher-to-child communication should still be in total communication, with every word said and signed.

The following careful communication habits should also be expected from oral children: (a) consistent attempts at precise speech; and (b) consistent attempts to communicate in English sentences. To establish these habits, the teacher employs techniques that are similar to those used with the total communication child. The teacher is careful to always:

1. model clear speech;
2. let the child know careless speech is unacceptable by cueing, then expecting, a more precise production; and
3. enthusiastically praise careful communiation attempts, letting the child know such habits are highly valued.

A teacher who requires, cues, and praises careful communication helps his students develop precise speech and signing skills that significantly contribute to their English proficiency.

Adult-to-adult communication

A maximum amount of adult-to-adult total communication should be encouraged in the school setting whenever hearing-impaired children are present. In learning about their language, normally hearing children derive great benefit from observing its application by adults; the same is true for hearing-impaired children. Therefore, any adult with signing skills should take the time to use them when hearing-impaired children are present. The teacher's responsibility is to encourage this use of total communication with school-related

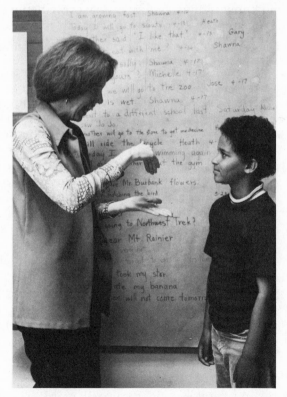

The Again Technique is enjoyable and helpful to hearing-impaired children. The classroom teacher is helping Christopher with a complete sentence.

people including: (a) other teachers of the hearing impaired; (b) classroom assistants in the program; (c) support staff, such as communication disorders specialists, audiologists, and psychologists; (d) volunteers; and (e) student teachers. Although classroom visitors will not always have signing skills, the teacher should still sign when speaking to them in front of children. A teacher who sets a good example and encourages speech and signs from other adults establishes a maximum amount of adult-to-adult total communication in the presence of hearing-impaired children.

Child-to-child communication

Hearing-impaired children should be encouraged to use total communication with each other. The teacher cannot assume children will always communicate in English sentences to each other, using speech with each word. She can, however, establish these habits as soon as a child enters the classroom, regardless of his level. When a teacher observes one child saying or signing partial sentences to another, she stops the child and tells him to use good sentences. Then, if the child needs assistance with his English, she builds a complete sentence with him using the Again Technique. Next, she tells him to direct the correct sentence to the other child. Afterwards, she praises him, making him proud of his sentence. Teacher praise also encourages the child to make similar attempts in the future when communicating with his peers. Parents can use the same approach with their child outside the school setting. After repeated correction and praise, in school and at home, children will start to use careful sentences with their peers independently.

Using Specific Instructional Techniques

The Again Technique

The Again Technique has been helpful in stimulating the development of English for hearing-impaired children. To use this technique, the teacher follows one of two similar procedures. The first is used with any child introduced to the Again Technique, including preschoolers or children of any age new to the teacher's classroom. The second procedure is used with children who are above preschool age and experienced in the Again Technique. Both basic procedures are nearly identical, since all steps are the same except the one that specifically involves building a complete sentence (Step 2).

Procedure I. Used with children introduced to the Again Technique. The first procedure involves eight steps.

Step 1. The child (C) initiates an incorrect production. This could include pointing, a partial sentence, or an incorrect sentence.

- *Example.* C: "Did she made it from Christmas?"

Step 2. The teacher (T) builds a complete, correct sentence with the child, using one word at a time.

- *Example.* T: "Did"
  - C: "Did"
  - T: "she"
  - C: "she"
  - T: *"make"* (emphasize by stressing word)
  - C: "make"
  - T: "it"
  - C: "it"
  - T: *"for"*
  - C: "for"
  - T: "Christmas?"
  - C: "Christmas?"

Step 3. The teacher says and signs the word "Again."

- *Example.* T: "Again . . . . . . Did" (Teacher cues first word, "Did." and can also cue second word, "she.")

Step 4. The child attempts the sentence, saying and signing each word.

- *Example.* C: "Did she make it from . . . "

Step 5. If an error is made, the teacher corrects by quickly interrupting the child.

- *Example.* T: *"for"*
  - C: "for"
  - T: "Christmas?"
  - C: "Christmas?"

Step 6. The teacher says and signs the word "Again."

- *Example.* T: "Again . . . . . . Did" (Teacher cues first word, "Did." and can also cue second word, "she.")

Step 7. The child repeats the sentence correctly.

- *Example.* C: "Did she make it for Christmas?"

Step 8. The teacher praises the child.

- *Example.* T: "Good sentence!"

An Again Technique sequence is considered complete when the child says the entire sentence independently, with no help from the teacher other than his cueing the first word or two in the sentence. This independent performance must be the child's second production of the sentence, at least, since her first was a direct imitation of the teacher's model, one word at a time. The teacher must cue an independent production by saying the word "Again." Any time the child's attempt at an independent production has to be corrected by the teacher, the instruction "Again," cueing one more attempt, must follow. Additional dialogue or directions should not be added because they may confuse or distract the child from the target sentence. Table 4.1 outlines the steps of Procedure I of the Again Technique.

TABLE 4.1
Procedure 1 of the Again Technique

1.	Child production—incorrect.
2.	Teacher builds correct sentence *one word at a time,* as child imitates, *one word at a time.*
3.	Teacher says, "Again."
4.	Child repeats sentence, makes error.
5.	Teacher corrects *one word at a time,* as child imitates *one word at a time.*

This step is variable. The three-step sequence (4, 5, 6) may not occur or may be used one or more times.

---

6. Teacher says, "Again."

---

7. Child makes correct production. (If child makes error, go back to step 5.)

---

8. Teacher praises child.

Procedure II. Used with children experienced in the Again Technique. Procedure II involves eight steps.

Step 1. The child (C) initiates an incorrect production or partial sentence.

- *Example.* C: "Did she made it from Christmas?"

Step 2. The teacher (T) says and signs the complete sentence correctly, followed by the child's imitation of that sentence.

- *Example.* T: "Did she *make* it *for* Christmas?"
  C: "Did she make it for Christmas?"

Step 3. The teacher says and signs "Again."

- *Example:* T: "Again." (May cue first word, "Did.")

Step 4. The child attempts the sentence, saying and signing each word.

- *Example.* C: "Did she make it from . . . "

Step 5. If an error is made, as above, the teacher corrects by interrupting the child, then repeating the entire sentence, followed by the child's imitation of that sentence.

- *Example.* T: "Did she make it *for* Christmas?"
  C: "Did she make it for Christmas?"

Step 6.　　The teacher says and signs, "Again."

- *Example.* T: "Again." (May cue first word, "Did.")

Step 7.　　The child repeats the sentence correctly.

- *Example.* C: "Did she make it for Christmas?"

Step 8.　　The teacher praises the child.

- *Example.* T: "Good sentence!"

As is the case with children beginning the Again Technique, a sequence is considered complete when the child says the entire sentence independently, with no help from the teacher. For experienced children, the first word in the sentence, at *most*, should be cued. This independent performance must be the child's second production of the sentence, at least, since his first complete sentence was a direct imitation of the teacher's model. For this reason, the teacher must say and sign "Again," even if the child has just imitated the entire sentence correctly. If the child's imitation is incorrect, the teacher must repeat the entire sentence and get the child's correct imitation before saying and signing "Again" to cue the final, independent, production. Any error in the child's independent production must be corrected once more by the teacher: (a) saying and signing the entire sentence; (b) getting a correct imitation by the child; and (c) saying, "Again." Additional dialogue or directions should not be added, since they may confuse or distract the child from the target sentence.

Table 4.2 outlines the steps of Procedure II of the Again Technique.

TABLE 4.2
Procedure II of the Again Technique

1.	Child production—incorrect.
2.	Teacher says and signs complete sentence correctly; child imitates whole sentence.

3.	Teacher says and signs, "Again."

4.	Child repeats sentence, makes error.

	This step is variable. The three-step sequence (4, 5, 6) may not occur or may be used one or more times.

5.	Teacher says and signs complete sentence correctly; child imitates whole sentence.

6.	Teacher says and signs, "Again."

7.	Child makes correct production. (If child makes error, go back to step 5.)

8.	Teacher praises child.

The Again Technique should also be used to correct imprecise speech or signing for a child who is capable of more accurate output. Prodedures I and II should be applied to speech and signing errors in the same way that they are applied to errors in English sentences. For example, assume that the words "made" and "for" were pronounced incorrectly or signed imprecisely. To correct, the teacher would model the accurate speech production or sign. This would be followed by the child's imitation of the model. Next, the teacher would cue an independent production by saying "Again," and the sequence would be considered complete when the child says the entire sentence independently with correct speech and signing.

Comparative data. Tables 4.3, 4.4, and 4.5 contain spontaneous sentences of two children who have had the Again Technique and two who have not. Correct and incorrect English sentence production will be contrasted between these two groups. Each child has a profound hearing loss. The age difference between the two groups of children should be noted; those who have not had the Again Technique are 12 years old, and those who have had it are 6 years old. The latter group has worked with the Again Technique since age 4. All sentences in the tables were produced spontaneously, with no help from the teacher. The samples are small, but they represent typical incorrect and correct sentences made by these children.

While examining the tables, pay close attention to the contrast between the sentences produced by children who have had the Again Technique and those sentences produced by children without the Again Technique. The sentences of the younger children, who have had the Again Technique, are more complex than those of the older children who have not had the Again Technique, for both correct and incorrect productions. Furthermore, the error sentences of the former group tend to approximate correct English grammar more than do those of the latter group.

Table 4.5 shows a 2-year period of growth in English sentences produced by the two Again Technique children of Table 4.3 and 4.4. It documents typical growth that occurs in the sentence production of hearing-impaired children who constantly work with the Again Technique. As 4-year-olds, these children started to produce simple English sentences after several months' work with the Again Technique. The data on Table 4.5 show all the sentences the children produced during the remaining 6 months of the school year. They were not producing exceptional sentences when the Again Technique was begun with them, but by age 6, with consistent application of the Again Technique, they were producing sentences quite exceptional for their age. Table 4.5 data are a very small sampling of the total number of correct English sentences the 6-year-olds produced over a 3-month period. This kind of growth is typical of children who have had consistent correction and work with the Again Technique.

TABLE 4.3
Sample of Incorrect English Sentence Attempts

Children with Again Technique		Children without Again Technique	
Child 1 (Age 6)	Child 2 (Age 6)	Child 3 (Age 12)	Child 4 (Age 12)
1. I have a new guns.	1. I have a dolls.	1. Bee is dead.	1. I more late.
2. (Child's name) know yesterday was Monday.	2. I am going to swim in the May.	2. How spell ugly?	2. I not cheat.
3. I have strong man.	3. I saw (child's name) is funny with her hands.	3. What is that for book?	3. Myself dream.
4. What color my scarf?	4. I do not go to church yesterday.	4. I went ice cream yesterday.	4. Old lady fat.
5. (Child's name) is not watching at me.	5. I am going to the doctor eye on Friday.	5. I not finished to read.	5. What mean?
6. Where did (child's name) went.			6. Can't find.
7. My mommy make it.			7. Do you have pen black?
			8. Stop! I can feel bother me.
			9. That girl bad.

52

TABLE 4.4
Sample of Correct English Sentences

Children with Again Technique		Children without Again Technique	
Child 1 (Age 6)	Child 2 (Age 6)	Child 3 (Age 12)	Child 4 (Age 12)
1. The man is fixing my hearing aid.	1. Is this mine?	1. I am cold.	1. Spell ugly.
2. My mother said we have enough books.	2. I am going on the bus later.	2. I have a good idea.	2. Understand?
3. My mommy and daddy will go far away to see a deer.	3. I went to the store on Saturday.	3. That's dry.	3. Hurry up! Hurry up!
4. Who will take the calendar home?	4. I will not tell Mommy.	4. May I have a different spoon?	4. My father won't.
5. Maybe I will go camping on Saturday.	5. Are the children painting?	5. I saw her brother.	5. Don't tell her please.
6. I have to wait for (child's name).	6. (Teacher's name), I will get bigger.		
7. My father told me I will have a birthday.	7. I saw (child's name) spill his milk.		
	8. My hearing aid is fixed now.		
	9. My mother painted my sister's room yesterday.		

Note. These are spontaneous sentences in total communication with no help from teacher.

53

TABLE 4.5
Growth in English Sentence Production

	Child 1 (Age 4)			Child 2 (Age 4)
2/12	Yes, I want more milk.		1/31	(Child's name) is there.
2/26	I want (child's name).		2/4	(Child's name) is sick.
2/27	I want (child's name).		2/27	I have a sweater.
3/4	(Child's name) is sick. I am first.		2/28	I am first.
			3/10	(Child's name) is sick. (Child's name) is sick. I am first.
3/5	Daddy is working.			
			3/19	(Child's name) is first.
3/7	Daddy is working.		3/25	(Child's name) is first.
3/26	Daddy is working.		4/8	(Child's name) is first.
3/28	I want more milk.		4/9	(Child's name) is sick.
4/10	I am sitting.		4/15	(Teacher's name) is sick.
4/24	I have a fish.			
			4/16	(Child's name) is bad.
4/25	(Child's name), please move.		4/25	I want to talk to (child's name).
			6/2	(Child's name) is first.
4/25	I have a fish.			
4/29	I have two mittens.			
5/1	I have purple.			
5/2	(Child's name) is in there. I have flowers.			
5/13	I am sitting.			
5/16	I want to see.			
5/20	I have a new hat.			
5/21	I am quiet.			
6/3	I want to go to the Space Needle.			
6/5	(Child's name), don't touch my coat.			
6/6	You are silly. I want to play with the game.			
6/9	I have a new hat.			
6/11	I don't know.			
6/12	I want some paper. Where is (child's name)?			

Child 1 (Age 6)		Child 2 (Age 6)	
9/17	The man is fixing my hearing aid.	9/15	Is this mine?
9/20	I have three peaches at home.	9/22	I am going on the bus later.
9/27	I was watching (child's name).	9/25	I went to the store on Saturday.
10/2	My daddy is here.	9/28	I am watching you.
10/9	I was hiding.	10/2	My mommy will come tomorrow.
10/16	May I put my mouse in my bag?	10/3	May I go to the bathroom please?
10/23	I will clean the table.	10/12	I will not come tomorrow.
10/30	(Child's name) is in the bathroom.	10/15	I have apple juice.
11/6	My mommy and daddy will go far away to see a deer.	10/28	May I wash my hands?
11/13	I have to wait for (child's name).	11/4	I found the red feather on the grass yesterday.
11/20	Mommy has many, many flowers at home from grandmother.	11/11	Are the children painting?
11/22	My father told me I will have a birthday.	11/16	You will change it today.

Note. These are spontaneous sentences in total communication with no help from teacher.

Practical application of the Again Technique. The Again Technique is appropriate throughout the entire school day. It may be used during both structured and unstructured situations. The teacher will not be able to apply the Again Technique to every incorrect sentence; it would be impractical due to time considerations of the daily schedule. The teacher has only a limited amount of time for each lesson plan, and thus has to decide how much time can be spent on interruptions. She should, however, try to correct as many sentences as possible throughout the entire school day.

Cueing

Cueing is a technique used in both spontaneous and structured situations; it helps a child give a correct answer he cannot give independently. A cue is a hint from the teacher to the child. The teacher must take care to give the child as much help as he needs to prevent frustration with the task, giving only as much help as necessary and allowing the child the opportunity to solve problems by himself. To accomplish this, the teacher can use various cues. They range from those that are actually the complete answer to be imitated by the child to those that are only partial prompts. The following is a list of cues and ways to use them with children. The cues are ordered according to the degree of teacher help involved, beginning with the most assistance and moving to the least.

Cue 1: Teacher helps child make response. The teacher may have to physically assist a very young child or one who is beginning a difficult new skill. For example, a teacher positions the fingers of a child having trouble forming a particular sign; or a teacher helps a child learn to print by grasping the pencil with the child, and guiding her letter formation. This type of cue requires the greatest amount of teacher involvement.

Cue 2: Teacher models response and child imitates. The next type of cue is a teacher model of a response the child imitates. For example, if a child has pronounced a word incorrectly, the teacher says the word correctly and asks the child to imitate it; or a teacher provides a child with a sign she does not know by correctly modelling it and requiring an imitation. If the child cannot imitate a desired response, the teacher must go back to Cue 1.

Cue 3: Teacher gives beginning of response. To use this cue, the teacher gives the child the initial portion of the response. For example, if a child has forgotton how to articulate a word she is signing, the teacher forms his lips into the initial position of the word.

This prompt helps the child remember how to pronounce the entire word. A teacher also partially cues the first word of the sentence to be repeated by using the Again Technique. He presents the beginning position of the first sign in that sentence. If the child cannot remember a desired response after a partial cue has been given, the teacher must go back to Cue 2.

Cue 4: Teacher nods head "yes" or "no". The teacher can cue by nodding his head "yes" or "no" in the following two situations: (a) If a child starts to make a desired response, but hesitates due to uncertainty, the teacher immediately shakes his head "yes," encouraging her to continue with the correct answer; (b) If the teacher feels the child can correct her own error by thinking about the answer more carefully, he interrupts the error response by clearly shaking his head "no." Cue 4 cuts off the child's error response and results in her search for a better answer. This cueing technique is more subtle than those techniques explained previously because no part of the desired response is contained in the cue. If the head nod cue is insufficient help, the teacher should go back to Cue 3.

Cue 5: Teacher uses facial expression. When instructing hearing-impaired children, the teacher continually uses facial expressions. But Cue 5 (facial expression) involves a more subtle technique. The teacher can use facial expressions as cues in the following three situations: (a) If a child starts to make a desired response, but hesitates due to uncertainty, the teacher uses a positive facial expression, such as a smile, encouraging the child to continue with the correct answer. This smile is used in place of the "yes" head nod if the teacher feels a more subtle cue would suffice; (b) If the teacher feels a child can correct her own error by thinking about the answer more carefully, he interrupts the error response by using a negative facial expression, such as a frown, signalling the child to look for a better answer. This frown is used in place of the "no" head nod if the child is capable of responding to a more subtle cue; and (c) If a child hesitates before completing a desired response, the teacher uses an expectant facial expression, alerting the child that additional output is required. Thus, the teacher encourages the child to think further about how to finish her answer. If the facial expression cue is insufficient help, the teacher must go back to Cue 4.

Fading cues

Fading cues is a process by which prompts are gradually eliminated. Initially, the teacher uses cues when a child shows uncertainty in responding. He keeps in mind, however, that the principal goal is to enable the child to respond independently, without the aid of cues. If the teacher judges that dropping cues all at once might cause confusion, he must lead the child to independence in a step-by-step process by gradually dropping parts of cues. As the cues are phased out, the child becomes more responsible for the task. Fading the cues must be done skillfully. It should not be paced too quickly, because the child is then given more task-responsibility than she can manage, and is frustrated. However, the process should move quickly enough to allow the child as much independence as she is ready to take on. For example, a teacher may be helping a child remember a particularly difficult sign by applying Cue 2; that is, modelling the sign for the child to imitate. The fading of this cue proceeds in the following steps, each step being used after the child shows mastery at the previous one.

1. When the teacher feels the child is ready, he uses Cue 3, giving only the beginning hand configuration of the sign to prompt the child.

2. Next, the teacher moves his hands toward the beginning position of the sign, as the partial cue.

3. The teacher then moves his hands in toward his body, giving no part of the sign.

4. Finally, the teacher drops all cues, letting the child respond independently.

At any time during the four-step series, if a child makes an error that she cannot correct independently, the teacher must go back one step.

As another example of fading cues, the same procedure can apply to fading a speech cue, either for the oral child or for the child using total communication. The teacher might be prompting the word "food" by using Cue 2; that is, by modelling the word for the child to imitate. The fading of this cue proceeds in the following steps, each step being used after the child shows mastery at the previous one.

1. When the teacher feels the child is ready, he moves to Cue 3, giving only the beginning sounds of the word to prompt the child. He says, "foo. . .".

2. The teacher then cues with the initial phoneme only. He says, "/f/".

3. Next, the teacher forms his lips in the initial phoneme position, but makes no sounds.

4. The teacher could follow by pointing to his lips, reminding the child of past cues.

5. Finally, the teacher drops all cues, letting the child respond independently.

At any time during the procedure, if a child makes an error that she cannot correct independently, the teacher must go back one step. The fading technique is appropriate for any cue, whether it is used during spontaneous language times or during structured lessons.

Correcting errors

When a child makes an error response, the teacher should correct him with a cue, followed by his immediate imitation of the answer. Then the teacher requires a more independent repetition from him. A series of 3 steps is appropriate for correcting any error.

1. First, the teacher cues the correct response. She should try to give the least amount of help necessary to elicit a correct answer from the child.

2. Next, the teacher says and signs, "Again," to elicit a more independent response from the child.

3. If the child makes an error in the independent repetition, the teacher goes back through Steps 1 and 2, until the child's independent response is correct.

These correction procedures are appropriate for a variety of errors, including, but not limited to, errors in speech, syntax, the formation of signs and fingerspelled letters, written work, spelling, and specific vocabulary.

If any of the skills listed are taught through a drill method, one more step is required in the correction procedure. This additional step needs to be applied only to lessons involving drill. Refer to the three-step correction procedure previously listed. When a correction is made during drill, Step 4 should be added.

4. After the original error has been corrected through Steps 1, 2, and 3, the teacher goes to the next drill item. After its completion, the teacher returns to the previous error item. If the child makes

the error again, the teacher corrects, using Steps 2, 3, and 4. If the child is correct, the teacher moves to another drill item.

For example, the teacher can apply this correction procedure when drilling a child on math facts. The teacher might have a packet of flash cards, each containing one math fact. If the child makes an error on the card, "7 + 5," the teacher would correct him by: (a) Step 1 cueing the answer, "12"; (b) Step 2 saying and signing, "Again," and showing the card one more time. If the child is correct, the teacher goes to (c) Step 4 presenting the next card, such as "9 + 4." After the child successfully answers, the teacher presents card "7 + 5" one more time. If he makes an error, she corrects by repeating Steps 2, 3, and 4. When the child correctly answers the "7 + 5" card, the teacher moves to a new card, such as "8 + 6." This series of correction steps would be appropriate for any error, whether the child made it during spontaneous language times or structured lessons.

Backward chaining

Backward chaining is an effective technique for teaching English sentence patterns in the language curriculum. While it is used for building sentences, the Again Technique is used for correcting them. Backward chaining is especially important with preschoolers or children of any age starting in a curriculum of complete English sentences, who have difficulty remembering word order. The technique involves teaching from the end of the sentence to the beginning, so that cueing one word in the sentence sets off a chain reaction that elicits the rest of the sentence. These procedures are used in starting the children on the Syntax Curriculum to be detailed later in this text. Since the first sentence pattern taught in this curriculum is "This is a/an noun," it will be used in the following example of the backward chaining steps.

Step 1.   Teach the last word of the sentence by having the child name objects or pictures of vocabulary words in a current unit.

 • *Example.* Teacher: Points to object or picture (cues if necessary).
   Child: "_____ ." (Identifies object or picture in one word.)

Step 2.   When the child is consistently and independently naming objects or pictures in a vocabulary unit, the teacher moves to the next word in the sentence.

- *Example.* Teacher: Cues "a"; then points to object or picture.
  Child: "a _____." (Identifies several objects or pictures.)

Step 3. When the child is consistently and independently saying and signing "a _____," the teacher moves to the next word in the sentence.

- *Example.* Teacher: Cues "is" and partially cues "a."
  Child: "is a _____." (Identifies several objects or pictures.)

Step 4. When the child is consistently and independently saying and signing "is a _____," the teacher moves to the next word in the sentence.

- *Example.* Teacher: Cues "This" and partially cues "is."
  Child: "This is a _____." (Identifies a number of objects or pictures.)

This sequence could be used over a varied period of time, from a few days to several weeks, depending on the child's abilities. The criterion for moving to a new step is the child's independent accomplishment of the current step. Procedures for correcting errors and cueing, previously described in this chapter, should be used as needed when you use backward chaining.

Drill procedures

Drill is a technique for efficiently presenting a set of material to the child. In drill exercises, the teacher or assistant quickly shows the child a series of task items one after another. For example, a teacher might want to drill a child on printed word recognition. The teacher would prepare a packet of cards, each containing one target word, to show to the child, one at a time. After each presentation, the child attempts to read the target word. The teacher corrects any error by using the procedures outlined previously in the section on correcting errors during drill. Drill exercises move along quickly. The child is told an answer if she cannot produce it within a short period of time. The following subject areas are among those that would be appropriately taught using drill: (a) printed vowel and consonant sounds; (b) vocabulary words; (c) sentence patterns; (d) printed words; (e) alphabet letters; (f) math tasks, such as counting, numeral recognition, and facts; and (g) spelling words. The teacher can use drill techniques with any subject containing a series of task items that can be dealt with by brief questions and answers.

Review procedures

The teacher should have a system for reviewing those subjects taught throughout the year. For any lesson, the teacher determines which information the children must master. Her expectations may not be the same for all. In some subject areas, children are expected to master all the lesson components; for example, they are expected to master each word in a vocabulary unit. In other subject areas, children will be required to master only the most important concepts and facts; for example, in a health lesson on food and nutrition, they are expected to memorize the four basic food groups. Only the mastery information need be included in periodic review. Since systematic review allows the teacher to determine which material the children have retained and which information must be retaught, it is of great value.

Children can do their review lessons independently or they can be directed by the teacher or assistant. There are two categories of independent review work. The first type involves seatwork the child performs independently, corrected and checked by the teacher or assistant. The teacher should plan a block of time for this type of review in the daily schedule. Concurrently, the teacher and assistant can work with children individually through tutoring or drill work. The second type of independent review work involves work planned and sent home by the teacher for the child to do with parental cooperation. Depending on the child's capability and age, and the type of homework, the parent will either work with the child or will see that he finishes the work and returns it to school.

Review lessons directed by the teacher or assistant can involve two procedures. The first is a check to see which mastery information the child has retained; straightforward drill can accomplish this goal. In the second procedure, any mastery information the child has forgotten is retaught by the teacher, using the Again Technique. Data must be kept on the child's errors so the teacher can check the child's corrected response the next day. If the child answers correctly on the first presentation, the review procedure is considered complete. If the child makes an error again, the same correction procedure involving the Again Technique and another presentation of the material the next day is continued until the child answers correctly on the first presentation of a particular day. This second procedure should not be used if the child has retained all the mastery information of a particular unit.

Positive reinforcement

Positive reinforcement techniques are used to reward the child for good behavior and accomplishments and to encourage the same kind of behavior in the future. The teacher commonly uses two types in the classroom: (a) social, such as praise, smiles, and hugs; and (b) material, such as stickers and stars. Food rewards should be used sparingly, if at all, unless a special behavior program is set up. The regular and consistent use of positive reinforcement is crucial for the teacher who wishes to create and maintain an enjoyable, productive learning environment. A skillful teacher, who manages a carefully structured and well disciplined classroom, uses continual positive feedback for at least three reasons: (a) teacher praise helps the child develop self confidence and gives her pride in classroom accomplishments; (b) consistent reinforcement from the teacher establishes a positive classroom atmosphere; and (c) if the teacher is delighted over the child's successes, no matter how small, the child will share his delight. Positive reinforcement increases the child's motivation to learn and succeed.

A skillful teacher maintains and balances structure and discipline with positive feedback and encouragement. This balance creates a positive learning environment where both children and teachers are motivated, productive, and successful.

PART
3

The Language Curriculum

Evaluating Language

Beginning and End-of-Year Evaluations

At the beginning and end of the school year, the teacher completes a formal assessment of each child, testing academic and nonacademic areas. The results of these tests are compared to monitor each child's growth. English language development and speech skills are two of the major areas tested at these times. The measures used for evaluating English development are a comprehensive vocabulary test and two language samples, one from a structured and another from a non-structured situation. Speech skills are evaluated with a phonetic inventory, testing the child's ability to produce phonemes in isolation, words, and connected speech.

Throughout the year, the teacher informally evaluates children on sentence patterns and speech. Every day, the teacher monitors their speech production, correct English sentences, and incorrect English. This ongoing process is necessary in order to coordinate individualized teaching with children's progress in speech and English development.

Expressive vocabulary test—curriculum-referenced

How to devise. This vocabulary test is devised directly from the classroom vocabulary units, which are groupings of nouns, verbs, adjectives, and adverbs taught throughout the year. All these vocabulary words are written on a master list; they are then catagorized by units on a test form that has boxes for recording correct and incorrect words over several years. Due to space considerations, only 3 or 4 years can be charted in one test packet; two or three packets will therefore be used throughout the child's elementary years. A picture card is designed to correspond to each vocabulary word. Sets of cards and packets of recording forms are produced in quantity; each teacher has one complete set of cards to be used every time she gives the test. Each child has a test packet kept in his file as he moves from grade to grade.

How to administer.   The teacher shows the child one card at a time in the order the words appear on the recording form. The child is directed to say and sign each word pictured. Each response is noted by the teacher in one of four ways.

1. *TO* means a total communication response; that is, the child signed the word and said it intelligibly.

2. *TU* is also a total communication response in which the child signed the word but said it unintelligibly.

3. *O* (oral) means the child said the word intelligibly and used no signs.

4. "-" means there was an error—the child either did not answer or gave the wrong sign or word.

After the test has been administered, scores are tallied.

A sample test is shown in Table 5.1. It is a page from an expressive vocabulary test recording packet. The left column lists vocabulary words to be tested and to their right are six columns for recording the child's responses. Two columns are used per year, for fall and spring testing; therefore, this table has enough recording spaces for 3 years. Before the test is administered, the teacher dates the appropriate column on each page of the recording packet. After the test has been given, the teacher tallies *TU*s, *O*s, *TO*s, and -s for each page, and notes the totals at the bottom of each column.

Table 5.2 is a summary page used to record the total number of *TU*s, *O*s, *TO*s, and -s for each test administration. Each section has a place for recording the testing date, total scores, and comments. Two sections are used per year for fall and spring testing; therefore, test scores for 3 years can be included in the summary page.

Language sample

Structured situation.   The teacher has a set of pictures to be used for stimulating English sentence productions; one set is designed for preschool and kindergarten, another for primary grades, and a third for intermediate grades. As the children advance, the test pictures

TABLE 5.1

Sample Expressive Vocabulary Test

Sample Vocabulary Words	Fall (1st year preschool)	Spring (1st year preschool)	Fall (1st year K)	Spring (1st year K)	Fall (1st year 1st grade)	Spring (1st year 1st grade)
dress	–	TU	TU	TO		
shirt	–	TU	TU	TU		
pants	TU	TO	TO	TO		
socks	–	TU	–	TO		
shoes	TU	TO	TO	TO		
sweater	–	TO	TO	TO		
hearing aid	–	TU	–	TO		
pajamas	–	TU	–	TU		
underpants	–	TO	–	TO		
undershirt	–	TU	–	TU		
belt	–	TO	TO	TO		
glasses	–	TU	–	TO		
skirt	–	TU	–	TU		
coat	TU	TO	TO	TO		
* blouse	–	–	–	TO		
* slip	–	–	–	TU		
* slippers	–	–	–	TU		
* bathrobe	–	–	–	TO		
* circle	TU	TU	TU	TU		
* square	–	–	–	TU		
* rectangle	–	–	–	TU		
* triangle	–	–	–	TU		
* line	–	–	–	TO		
* curve	–	–	–	TO		
Totals	4 TU 20 –	6 TO 9 TU 9 –	5 TO 3 TU 16 –	14 TO 10 TU		

Note. *These words are not taught until kindergarten level.

TABLE 5.2
Sample Summary Page

Level: 1st year preschool
Date: month/day/year   *Totals*
Score: 36/462   0   TO
                          36   TU
Comments: 0   O
Only area of *strength*:   426   –
  Toy Vocabulary Words.
Also knew a few common
  words and signs.
	Level: 1st year preschool
	Date: month/day/year *Totals*
	Score: 161/462 53 TO
	                       108 TU
	Comments: 0 O
	Only areas of *weakness*: 301 –
	  furniture
	  money
	  summer } not taught yet
	  Kindergarten when tested
	  Level words

Note. 188 possible preschool words	*Note.* 188 possible preschool words

Level: 1st year kindergarten
Date: month/day/year   *Totals*
Score: 129/462   32   TO
                      97   TU
Comments: 0   O
Forgot many preschool 333   –
  vocabulary words over summer
  vacation
Many unintelligible responses
  with correct signs; speech
  deteriorated over summer
  vacation
	Level: 1st year kindergarten
	Date: month/day/year *Totals*
	Score: 361/462 197 TO
	                      164 TU
	Comments: 0 O
	Only areas of weakness: 101 –
	  materials
	  people } not taught yet
	  Kindergarten when tested
	  Level II words
	Significant increase in intelligible
	responses with correct signs

Level: _____ Date: _____ Score: _____ *Comments*	Level: _____ Date: _____ Score: _____ *Comments*

Note. 462 words in Expressive Vocabulary Test, but only 188 possible words at preschool level.

change; the number of pictures is increased, and they depict more complex activities. Children see these test pictures only during formal assessments at the beginning and end of the year.

The teacher presents one picture at a time to a child and says, "What is happening?" Then she records verbatim the first completed thought expressed by the child, typically, the first sentence attempted for each picture. A sample of at least 50 responses should be taken. After completing the test, the teacher scores responses by computing a mean length of response (MLR): she counts the number of words per sentence, adds these numbers, and divides by the total number of sentences to get the average number of words per sentence. The word "response" is used instead of the more traditional "utterance" (mean length of utterance) since the child's production may be by oral *or* visual modalities. Typical grammatical errors are also specified on the response sheet.

Non-structured situations. The teacher observes the child during a nonacademic time when children are allowed to converse freely with peers and teachers. He records verbatim the child's first 50

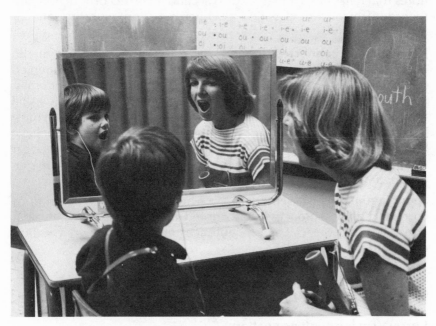

Speech work is a very important part of the total communication process. Heath enjoys his individual speech time.

productions. Production is defined as a sentence or phrase containing a complete thought. For more oral children, a tape recorder may be used and the sample transcribed later. The language sample is scored by computing a MLR as described previously.

Speech evaluations.   The teacher records the child's ability to produce each vowel and consonant sound in isolation. For younger children, or for those who have not yet learned to recognize printed symbols, the teacher says each sound, and asks the child to imitate it, until all sounds have been checked. Correct and incorrect imitations are noted. For children who have worked with printed symbols, vowel and consonant cards are used to elicit phoneme production.

Phonemes in words.   A formal or teacher-made test may be used to check sound production in initial, medial, and final positions in words. The test lists words that check the sounds in the various positions, and pictures that correspond to each word. The teacher presents a picture and asks the child to produce the corresponding word. If the child does not know the word, the teacher models it, and notes that it has been imitated. Correct and incorrect productions are recorded; errors are classified as either omissions, substitutions, or distortions.

Phonemes in connected speech.   As a less formal part of the evaluation, the teacher continually listens to the child's connected speech and notes the correct and incorrect production of phonemes. Producing phonemes in connected speech is a more complex skill than producing phonemes in isolation or in words; therefore, it must be monitored independently for phoneme errors that might not have been made in the simpler tasks. For the beginning- and end-of-year evaluations, the teacher documents correct and incorrect phoneme production in connected speech.

Spontaneous English sentences.   The child's ability to produce correct English sentences is also noted in the twice-yearly evaluations. Typical correct English sentences and common grammatical errors are documented.

Ongoing Evaluations

Correct English sentence patterns

Each child's growth in producing English sentences is monitored daily in the following way. The teacher draws a chart divided into columns on the blackboard for recording correct, spontaneous English sentences. Each child has a column with his name at the top and room for his correct sentences underneath (see Table 10.4, page 159). If the child initiates a sentence and says it correctly for the first time to a teacher or peer, it is written on the blackboard, and both child and teacher read the sentence together. At preschool level, the teacher reads, and the child follows along. At older levels, the children can read the sentences themselves. Their readings are always followed by praise.

If a spontaneous sentence is incorrect, the teacher builds it into a correct one with the child, using the Again Technique, detailed in Chapter 4. In this way, children learn that attempts at complete sentences are expected and praised, and they continually attempt to communicate in sentences. This method of evaluation also allows the teacher to monitor the child's daily growth in producing English sentences. One sentence per week is transferred to a permanent recording form kept with the child's academic records that are passed from teacher to teacher. Table 10.16, page 179 is an example of such a form.

Errors in English sentence patterns

Each child's errors in English are continually monitored in the following way. Throughout the week, the teacher writes down each child's incorrect, spontaneous sentences. Then, at least one of these sentences is transferred every week to a permanent recording form, kept with the child's academic records that are passed from teacher to teacher. Table 10.17, page 180 is an example of such a form. Error sentences are corrected through application of the Again Technique.

Correct and incorrect phonemes in connected speech

Each child's speech output is monitored daily, but it is recorded in the permanent records only at the beginning- and end-of-year evaluations. Errors in phoneme production are corrected through application of the Again Technique. Correct speech is praised regularly. In this way, the child continually has the opportunity to practice speech skills and to get constructive feedback.

Vocabulary

In the classroom, vocabulary words are taught in structured lessons and during non-structured, spontaneous language times. Vocabulary words that are taught during the structured times should be orga-

Patricia and Roxane are using total communication to discuss the current science unit with their classroom teacher.

nized into units. These fall into three main types: (a) classification units; (b) parts of speech units; and (c) survival word units. Reading and spelling are two other academic skills that are coordinated with the teaching of the vocabulary words, in all three types of units.

Teaching vocabulary words during non-structured times is often motivated by children's spontaneous communications. Whenever a child indicates confusion about a word, it needs to be explained. Other spontaneous teaching is motivated by the teacher, who may think of additional, related words that apply to a situation.

Structured lessons

Classification units.   Tables 5.3 and 5.4 contain sample vocabulary words which can be taught at the preschool, kindergarten, and early primary levels. The vocabulary words are grouped into units according to classification, such as toy words, body part words, clothing words, and classroom words. These units are possible examples of units that can be taught over an entire year, and can be expanded at the primary and intermediate levels by the addition of increasingly complex words.

TABLE 5.3
Preschool Vocabulary Units

Fall	Halloween	Body Parts	Winter
Level I	*Level I*	*Level I*	*Level I*
bus	witch	eye	snow
nut	owl	nose	snowman
squirrel	ghost	ear	ice
leaf	pumpkin	mouth	sled
tree	black cat	hair	boots
school	mask	arm	mittens
teacher	*Level II*	hand	coat
children	bat	leg	hat
Level II	Halloween	foot	*Level II*
rake	trick-or-treat	*Level II*	scarf
grass	**Animals**	finger	umbrella
Colors	*Level I*	toe	**Family**
Level I	dog	head	*Level I*
red	cat	back	mom
blue	cow		dad
yellow	horse	**Christmas**	brother
orange	fish	*Level I*	sister
green	snake	Christmas tree	grandma
purple	bird	present	grandpa
black	chicken	Santa Claus	*Level II*
brown	pig	reindeer	family
white	rabbit	star	**Clothing**
gray	monkey	candy cane	*Level I*
pink	elephant	*Level II*	dress
Level II	*Level II*	angel	shirt
gold	bear	stocking	pants
silver	giraffe	candle	socks
Vegetables	mouse	fireplace	shoes
Level I	kangaroo		sweater
corn	sheep	**Toys**	hearing aid
beans	spider	*Level I*	*Level II*
tomato	goat	ball	pajamas
celery	duck	airplane	underpants
lettuce	**Thanksgiving**	blocks	undershirt
carrot	*Level I*	doll	belt
Level II	pie	car	glasses
onion	Indian	tricycle	skirt
potato	turkey	boat	
peas	jello	*Level II*	
	tepee	balloon	
	Level II	puzzle	
	Thanksgiving	truck	
		tractor	

TABLE 5.3 (*cont.*)
Preschool Vocabulary Units

Prepositions	**Spring**	**Summer**
Level I	*Level I*	*Level I*
above	sun	swimming suit
below	flower	towel
in	butterfly	lake
on	bee	slide
ahead	seeds	swing
behind	kite	pool
Level II	caterpillar	*Level II*
under	*Level II*	beach
Textures	nest	picnic
Level I	egg	
soft	**Furniture**	
hard	*Level I*	
rough	bed	
smooth	chair	
sticky	t.v.	
Level II	sink	
expand	lamp	
meanings	rug	
in more	table	
contexts	refrigerator	
Fruit	stove	
Level I	*Level II*	
apple	mirror	
orange	curtains	
peach	dresser	
pear	couch	
banana	**Money**	
strawberry	*Level*	
grapes	quarter	
Level II	dollar	
lemon	dime	
blackberry	nickel	
	penny	
	money	
	Level II	
	expand	
	meanings	
	in more	
	contexts	

TABLE 5.4
Kindergarten/Primary Vocabulary Units

Fall
fall
school
teacher
children
bus
tree
leaf
grass
nut
squirrel
rake

Colors
red
blue
yellow
orange
green
purple
black
brown
white
gray
pink
gold
silver

Shapes
circle
square
rectangle
triangle
line
curve
whole
half

Classroom
Level I
desk
table
chair
pencil
crayon
hearing aid
glasses
chalk
chalkboard
paper
scissors
book
flag
paste
blocks
mirror
lights
wastepaper basket

Level II
eraser
pin
pen
paperclip
stapler
ruler
thumb tack
tape
rubberband
pencil-sharpener
room
floor

Size Relationships
big
little
more
less
small
large
long
short
tall

Halloween
Halloween
ghost
owl
pumpkin
jack-o-lantern
broom
black cat
moon
bat
mask
skeleton
witch
trick-or-treat
spider's web

Place Setting
Level I
plate
fork
knife
spoon
bowl
cup
glass
napkin

Level II
saucer
placemat
tablecloth
dishes

Foods
Breakfast
Level I
milk
juice
cereal
eggs
bread
toast

Level II
waffle
pancake
bacon
fruit
breakfast

Lunch
Level I
sandwich
cheese
soup
meat
crackers

Level II
hotdog
hamburger
french fries
potato chips
tuna fish
peanut butter
lunch

Dinner
Level I
meat
salad
potato
vegetable
bread

Level II
turkey
chicken
ham
gravy
baked potato
spaghetti
salt
pepper
sugar
food
dinner

TABLE 5.4 (*cont.*)
Kindergarten/Primary Vocabulary Units

Foods	Toys	Winter	Body Parts
Dessert	toys	winter	body
Level I	wagon	jacket	eye(s)
pie	boat	ice skates	nose
cake	ball	snow	ear(s)
cookies	airplane	ice	head
candy	balloon	hat	hair
Level II	tricycle	coat	mouth
ice cream	bicycle	scarf	face
cupcake	drum	mittens	back
donut	scooter	boots	arm(s)
jello	train	sweater	hand(s)
dessert	blocks	gloves	finger(s)
Thanksgiving	car	snowman	leg(s)
Thanksgiving	doll		foot
Indian	puzzle	**Clothing**	feet
feather	horn	*Level I*	toe(s)
turkey	truck	blouse	*Level II*
cranberries	tractor	pajamas	eyebrow
pumpkin pie		dress	eyelashes
pilgrim	**Christmas**	skirt	forehead
tepee	*Level I*	coat	lips(s)
Weather	Christmas	shoes	tooth
wind	Christmas tree	belt	teeth
windy	reindeer	pants	elbow(s)
sun	bell	shirt	wrist (s)
sunny	stocking	socks	knee(s)
fog	fireplace	sweater	ankle (s)
foggy	chimney	underpants	fingernail(s)
snow	candle	undershirt	toenail(s)
snowy	angel	*Level II*	**Materials**
snowing	present	slip	glass
rain	candy cane	panties	wood
rainy	star	shorts	rubber
raining	sled	slippers	cloth
cloud	Santa Claus	bathrobe	plastic
clouds	*Level II*		metal
cloudy	gift		cement
	ornament		
	wreath		
	ribbon		
	bow		
	log		

TABLE 5.4 (*cont.*)
Kindergarten/Primary Vocabulary Units

Prepositions	People	Farm Animals	House
in	people	farm	*Level I*
inside	girl	barn	house
out	boy	cow	door
outside	man	calf	floor
over	men	horse	rug
under	woman	colt	curtains
around	women	pony	key
above	lady	pig	T.V.
below	Mr.	goose	sink
on	Miss	duck	stove
off	Mrs.	sheep	refrigerator
beside	Ms.	lamb	window
between	friend	chicken	couch
ahead	children	hen	lamp
behind	**Spring**	rooster	bed
Family	spring	goat	pillow
Level I	umbrella		blanket
family	raincoat	**Zoo Animals**	dresser
mother	sun	zoo	soap
father	bee	lion	washcloth
sister	butterfly	tiger	toilet
brother	bird	elephant	bathtub
mommy	nest	zebra	hairbrush
daddy	kite	turtle	toothbrush
grandmother	seeds	snake	comb
grandma	flower	seal	*Level II*
grandfather	garden	camel	bedroom
grandpa	**Money**	kangaroo	livingroom
baby	money	bear	bathroom
cat	penny	monkey	kitchen
kitten	1 cent	giraffe	dining room
dog	nickel	**Summer**	closet
puppy	5 cents	summer	**Textures**
Level II	dime	swimming suit	soft
wife	10 cents	bathing suit	hard
husband	quarter	towel	smooth
son	25 cents	lake	rough
daughter	dollar	pool	sticky
aunt		beach	
uncle		slide	
cousin		swing	
		grass	
		picnic	

TABLE 5.4 (*cont.*)
Kindergarten/Primary Vocabulary Units

Vegetables
celery
potato
peas
beans
onion
corn
lettuce
carrots
tomato
vegetable

Fruits
banana
apple
orange
lemon
peach
pear
plum
grapes
blackberry
strawberry
raspberry
pineapple
fruit

Time
clock
watch
hour
time for school
time to play
time for lunch
time to go home

Special Days
Valentine's Day
valentine
heart
card
valentine party
"I love you"

Easter
Easter
Easter egg
rabbit
bunny
Easter basket
Easter egg hunt

Birthday
birthday
birthday card
birthday cake
birthday party
candles
presents

Parts-of-Speech units.   Table 5.5 contains sample units for various grade levels. Parts of speech are taught at every elementary level, and units are expanded from year to year by the teacher's addition of words, less frequently used synonyms, words with difficult meanings and words with multiple meanings. A variety of commercially-made materials that contain parts-of-speech word cards and corresponding pictures are available aids for teaching these units.

Survival vocabulary.   Table 5.6 contains sample survival-word vocabulary units. Survival words are common, practical words that are necessary in daily living; children should know these words expressively and be able to read them.

One method of determining survival words involves sets of lists containing high-frequency words found in common reading materials, such as texts, newspapers, and magazines. These sets are commercially available. One set should be chosen as a source of survival words. Next, the staff in a program for hearing-impaired children must consider all words, one by one, to determine which are crucial to elementary children in their daily living. These words are compiled into a separate list. Wherever possible, they are incorporated into

The daily schedule includes a time for individual work with the classroom assistant. Kim is being tutored individually in spelling.

TABLE 5.5
Parts of Speech Units

Verbs*	Adjectives*	Pronouns
Preschool/	Intermediate	Personal
Kindergarten	Sample	Pronouns
Sample	happy	I
swim	sad	you (singular)
walk	rough	he, she, it
cry	smooth	we
drink	strong	you (plural)
eat	weak	they
jump	wet	Objective
fall	dry	Pronouns
sit	hard	me
sleep	soft	you (singular)
skate	sick	her, him, it
sweep	well	us
run	fat	you (plural)
blow	thin	them
brush	young	Possessive Pronouns
climb	old	(modifiers)
fly	light	my
hide	heavy	your (singular)
kick	warm	his, her, its
pull	cool	our
push	real	your (plural)
ride	toy	their
throw	tall	Possessive Pronouns
wash	short	(subjects or complements)
write	full	mine
break	empty	yours (singular)
carry	new	his, hers, its
cough	old	ours
crawl	clean	yours (plural)
cut	dirty	theirs
dance	noisy	Intensive and Reflexive
drop	quiet	Pronouns
fight	straight	myself
sew	crooked	yourself
sneeze	high	himself, herself, itself
tear	low	ourselves
yawn	hungry	yourselves
	full	themselves
	light	
	dark	

*Note. These verbs and adjetives are taught throughout the school year.

TABLE 5.5 (cont.)
Parts of Speech Units

Adverbs	Degree and	Prepositions
Intermediate	*Measure*	*Kindergarten/Primary*
Sample	all	*Sample*
Manner	almost	in
alike	less	inside
so	little	out
worse	much	outside
Time and	quite	over
Succession	completely	under
when	equally	around
finally	*Assertion*	above
late	*Condition and*	below
soon	*Concession*	on
afterwards	yes	off
never	no	beside
Place and	certainly	between
Direction	not	ahead
far	perhaps	behind
there	possibly	
below	o.k.	
upstairs		
north		
south		
east		
west		
Cause and		
Purpose		
therefore		
consequently		

TABLE 5.6

Sample Survival-word Vocabulary Units

Nouns	Verbs	Adjectives	Adverbs
nothing	bring	right	why
something	shut	wrong	what
none	open	thirsty	when
some	close	open	where
bridge	tell	shut	who
fire	feel	bright	again
smoke	wait	much	yes
danger	smell	many	no
year	hear	more	now
month	listen	good	then
week	look	best	there
day	taste	better	since
hour	exit	smart	however
minute	enter	lovely	soon
second	explain	lazy	finally
doctor	touch	plenty	never
nurse	watch	enough	really
dentist	print	easy	nearly
restroom	write	safe	quickly
ticket	practice	awful	slowly
time	review	quiet	loudly
watch	answer	terrible	almost
clock	repeat	wonderful	less
inch	add	mad	much
foot	subtract	sorry	little
yard	multiply	deaf	all
age	divide	hard-of-hearing	perhaps
number	choose	true	possibly
letter	pick	false	
page	agree	both	
answer	disagree	round	
question	read	neat	
morning		messy	
afternoon		kind	
night		nice	
today		favorite	
yesterday		huge	
tomorrow		dead	
name		alive	
store			
office			
restaurant			
ground			
sky			
mistake			

previously established classification or parts-of-speech vocabulary units. The remaining survival words are grouped into units by parts of speech. Survival-word definitions and print recognition are taught at every elementary level.

Incorporating other skill areas.　　There is a progressive change in vocabulary units from year to year, with units from previous years expanded, and new units introduced each year. Teaching a complete unit usually takes from 1 to 2 weeks. Teachers include two other academic skills—reading and spelling—when teaching vocabulary units. Pre-reading skills and beginning sight-word recognition are covered at the preschool level. In each successive grade, more sight words must be mastered, and more decoding skills are developed. Spelling is formally introduced after the children can both recognize and print all alphabet letters from memory, usually in first-year primary. In each successive grade, spelling words of increased difficulty are added. The number of spelling words per test is also increased from year to year.

Non-structured, spontaneous lessons

Spontaneous vocabulary lessons can be motivated by the child or by the teacher. The child may indicate that he does not understand a word, either by incorrect usage, confusion, or inquiry. The teacher may initiate spontaneous discussions about unplanned vocabulary words that relate to a situation. A creative teacher will capitalize on these opportunities to enrich the classroom curriculum in imaginative ways.

Syntax Instruction

English syntax, or grammatically structured sentences, must be taught systematically to hearing-impaired children in both structured and non-structured lessons.

Structured Lessons

A practical English syntax curriculum

The following curriculum was written to develop hearing-impaired children's ability to communicate verbally. In most cases, total communication should be used. Occasionally, for a particular child, oral output not accompanied by signs will be accepted. (Appropriate communication methods for individual hearing-impaired children will be discussed in detail in Chapter 9.)

Most syntax curricula used with hearing-impaired children involve a written approach. Sentence patterns are either written by the child, formed by ordering word cards, or completed by filling in blanks. Then the child may read the sentence aloud. Reading and writing (or printing) are the two expressive skills practiced. The following curriculum was developed to improve verbal expressive skills not involving reading. A syntax curriculum using a verbal approach, rather than a written approach, was developed with the aim of improving verbal communication skills. This curriculum teaches these skills directly, because reading skills do not necessarily generalize to conversational skills. Another strength of this verbal approach is its usability with preschool children. Curriculum work on communication in correct English sentences can begin early, and can be continued by reviewing and expanding from year to year. This practical English syntax curriculum follows.

Introductory tasks

Most children should master the introductory section of the curriculum before the teacher starts instruction of the remainder. In some cases for older children, instruction may begin on both sections simultaneously. Introductory tasks involve following directions and answering questions with "yes" or "no," in that order. The directions are: 1) "Touch the _____ ."; 2) "Give me the _____ .": and 3) "Give him/her the _____ ." Yes/no questions to be answered are: 1) "Are you touching the _____ ?"; 2) "Is this a _____ ?"; and 3) "Are you (verb) ing?" Tasks are sequenced, and mastery on one is required before the child moves to the next. The following procedures shown on Table 6.1 should be used for teaching the introductory section.

TABLE 6.1
Introductory Section: English Syntax Curriculum

Teach the Introductory Tasks in the Following Order:
I. **Directions.**
    A.   Touch the _____ .
       1. Give direction, "Touch the _____ ," and move the child's hand if necessary to prompt.
       2. Using a small number of objects or pictures, fade the prompt.
       3. Criterion for mastery: Child follows the direction 100% of the time on 2 consecutive days, with no prompts. At least three different objects or pictures should be used each day.
    B.   Give me the _____ .
       1. Use same teaching steps as for "Touch the. _____ ."
       2. To prompt, teacher holds out hand.
       3. To fade prompt, teacher moves hand in toward body by degrees until prompt is dropped.
       4. Criterion for mastery is the same as for "Touch the _____ ."
    C.   Alternate "Touch the _____ ," and "Give me the _____ ' " until the child correctly follows the directions 100% of the time, on 2 consecutive days, with no prompts, using at least three different objects or pictures each day.
       CORRECTION: If the child has trouble with one particular direction, go back to step A or step B.
    D.   Present "Touch the _____ ," and "Give me the _____ ," randomly until the child correctly follows the directions 100% of the time on 2

consecutive days, with no prompts, using at least three different objects or pictures each day.

CORRECTION: If the child makes consistent errors, go back to step C.

E. "Give him/her the _____ ." (Note: The distinctions here are both between third person and/or first person [him/her and me] and between masculine and feminine pronouns [him and her]. Therefore trials must permit the child to select a person of the correct gender for him and her.)

1. Use the same teaching steps as for "Give me the _____ ."
2. To prompt, point to appropriate "him" or "her."
3. To fade prompt, move hand in toward body by degrees until prompt is dropped.
4. Criterion for mastery is the same as for "Give me the _____ ."

F. Alternate "Give him/her the _____ ," with "Touch the _____ ," as in step C.

G. Randomly present "Give him/her the ," and "Touch the _____ ," as in step D.

H. Alternate "Give him/her the _____ ," and "Give me the _____ ," as in step C.

I. Randomly present "Give him/her the _____ ," and "Give me the _____ ," as in step D.

J. Randomly present "Give him/her the _____ ," and "Give me the _____ ," and "Touch the _____ ," as in step D.

II. **Yes/No Tasks**

A. Are you touching the _____ ?

1. Using one or two objects or pictures, have the child touch one, and ask him, "Are you touching the _____ ?"
2. Prompt by modelling "yes" for the child.
3. To fade prompt, move hand in toward body by degrees until prompt is dropped.
4. Criterion for mastery: Child follows direction and answers "yes" 100% of the time on 2 consecutive days, with no prompts, using at least three different objects or pictures each day.
5. Ask the same question where the answer is "no." (Child is directed to touch one picture and asked if he is touching another.)
6. Prompt by modelling "no" if necessary.
7. Fade prompt in same way as in step 3.
8. Criterion for mastery: same as in step 4, with child answering "no" instead of "yes."
9. Alternate "yes" and "no" questions until the child correctly follows the directions and answers the questions 100% of the time, on 2 consecutive days, with no prompts, using at least three different objects or pictures each day.

CORRECTION: If the child makes consistent errors, go back to step 1 or step 5.

10. Randomly present "yes" and "no" questions until the child correctly follows the directions and answers the questions 100% of the time, on 2 consecutive days, with no prompts, using at least three different objects or pictures each day.

CORRECTION: If the child makes consistent errors, go back to step 9.

B. Is this a _____ ?

1. Teach with the same steps used in "Are you touching the _____ ?"

2. Use the same prompts, criteria for mastery, and corrections.

C. Are you (verb)ing?

1. Pick three verbs for this sentence pattern, such as:
"Are you sitting?"
"Are you standing?"
"Are you walking?"

2. Present each verb direction, one at a time, until child correctly follows direction 100% of the time, on 2 consecutive days, with no prompts.

3. Teach answer to "Are you (verb)ing?" in the same sequence used in step A ("Are you touching the _____ ?").

4. Use the same prompts, criteria for mastery, and corrections.

5. Present each verb direction, e.g., "sit," "stand," "walk," one at a time until child correctly follows direction 100% of the time, on 2 consecutive days, with no prompts.

6. Teach answer to "Are you (verb) ing?" in the same sequence used in step A ("Are you touching the _____ ?"), while the child is following a direction.

7. Use the same prompts, criteria for mastery, and corrections.

Table 6.1 contains ordered teaching steps for the introductory section of the English syntax curriculum. It is particularly important to follow these steps carefully with young children and with older ones who show confusion with the tasks. Any child first entering an elementary program for hearing-impaired children, regardless of her age, should be tested for mastery of the introductory section of the curriculum. Any tasks not accomplished can then be taught directly. It cannot be assumed that hearing-impaired children will know the meanings of specific directions, or answer yes/no questions correctly. It is the responsibility of the teacher to determine the child's abilities in these areas.

Syntax curriculum

Curriculum tasks involve learning to understand and produce a variety of English sentence patterns. Tasks are taught during tutoring time, and progress is recorded on charts kept in the tutoring area. Tables 10.1 and 10.2, Chapter 10 are examples. Sentences are organized by type into charts, usually with no more than eight per grouping. Charts are taught in a specific order, as the sentences comprising them. Sentences and charts should not be taught out of sequence, because mastery of one sentence pattern is the criterion for moving to the next. If in response to three different objects or pictures a child independently produces a pattern with no errors three times in a row, he is allowed to put a sticker on the chart near the sentence he has mastered. Then the teacher notes the date of mastery next to the sticker. Older children can also keep small copies of the charts in their desks, to use when they practice during free times. The following tables (Table 6.2 through Table 6.17) show the English sentence patterns, stepped out, grouped, and arranged according to teaching order.

They contain specific teacher questions and the precise answers expected from the child. These are for teacher reference. When these sentence patterns are on charts used with children, only the questions appear, so that the children will respond in a conversational way, rather than reading the answers. Refer to Tables 10.1 and 10.2, Chapter 10 for examples of the charts to be used with children. In addition, each child should have a data book containing the syntax curriculum charts on notebook paper. These should be filled out by the teacher as the child masters sentence patterns, and passed from grade to grade as part of her permanent records.

TABLE 6.2
Beginning Sentence Patterns*

Question	Answer
What is this?	This is a/an (<u>noun</u>).
Is this a/an (<u>noun</u>)?	Yes, this is a/an (<u>noun</u>).
What is that?	That is a/an (<u>noun</u>).
Is that a/an (<u>noun</u>)?	Yes, that is a/an (<u>noun</u>).
What do you have?	I have the (<u>noun</u>).
Do you have the (<u>noun</u>)?	Yes, I have the (<u>noun</u>).
What do you see?	I see a/an (<u>noun</u>).
Do you see a/an (<u>noun</u>)?	Yes, I see a/an (<u>noun</u>).

*Note. A variety of nouns should be used.

TABLE 6.3
Beginning Adjective Patterns*

Question	Answer
What is this?	This is a/an (adj.) (noun).
Is this a/an (adj.) (noun)?	Yes, this is a/an (adj.) (noun).
What is that?	That is a/an (adj.) (noun).
Is that a/an (adj.) (noun)?	Yes, that is a/an (adj.) (noun).
What do you have?	I have the (adj.) (noun).
Do you have the (adj.) (noun)?	Yes, I have the (adj.) (noun).
What do you see?	I see a/an (adj.) (noun).
Do you see a/an (adj.) (noun)?	Yes, I see a/an (adj.) (noun).

*Note. A variety of nouns and adjectives should be used.

TABLE 6.4
Beginning Verb Patterns*

Question	Answer
What is the boy/girl doing?	The boy/girl is (verb) ing.
Is the girl/boy (verb) ing?	Yes, the girl/boy is (verb) ing.
Who is (verb) ing?	The boy/girl is (verb) ing.
What is the girl/boy doing?	The girl/boy is (verb) ing the (noun).
Is the boy/girl (verb) ing the (noun)?	Yes, the boy/girl is (verb) ing the (noun).
Who is (verb) ing the (noun)?	The girl/boy is (verb) ing the (noun).
Can a boy/girl (verb)?	Yes, a boy/girl can (verb).
Can a girl/boy (verb) a (noun)?	Yes, a girl/boy can (verb) a (noun).

*Note. Contracted forms should be introduced in beginning primary grades.

92

TABLE 6.5
Beginning Negative Patterns*

Question	Answer
Is this a/an (noun)?	No, this is not a/an (noun).
Is that a/an (noun)?	No, that is not a/an (noun).
Do you have the (noun)?	No, I do not have the (noun).
Do you see a/an (noun)?	No, I do not see a/an (noun).
Is the girl/boy (verb) ing?	No, the girl/boy is not (verb) ing.
Is the boy/girl (verb) ing the (noun)?	No, the boy/girl is not (verb) ing the (noun).
Can a girl/boy (verb)?	No, a girl/boy cannot (verb).
Can a boy/girl (verb) a (noun)?	No, a boy/girl cannot (verb) a (noun).

*Note. Contracted forms should be introduced in beginning primary grades.

TABLE 6.6
Beginning Sentence Patterns—Plurals in Object*

Question	Answer
What are these?	These are (noun) s.
Are these (noun) s?	Yes, these are (noun) s.
What are those?	Those are (noun) s.
Are those (noun) s?	Yes, those are (noun) s.
What do you have?	I have the/some (noun) s.
Do you have the/some (noun) s?	Yes, I have the/some (noun) s.
What do you see?	I see the/some (noun) s.
Do you see the/some (noun) s?	Yes, I see the/some (noun) s.

*Note. A variety of nouns should be used.

TABLE 6.7
Beginning Sentence Patterns—Plurals in Subject*

Question	Answer
What are the boys/girls doing?	The boys/girls are (verb) ing.
Are the girls/boys (verb) ing?	Yes, the girls/boys are (verb) ing.
Who is (verb) ing?	The boys/girls are (verb) ing.
What are the girls/boys doing?	The girls/boys are (verb) ing the (noun).
Are the boys/girls (verb) ing the (noun)?	Yes, the boys/girls are (verb) ing the (noun).
Who is (verb) ing the (noun)?	The girls/boys (verb) ing the (noun).
Can girls/boys (verb) a (noun)?	Yes, girls/boys can (verb) a (noun).

*Note. A variety of nouns and verbs should be used.

TABLE 6.8
Compound Subject—Present Tense*

Question	Answer
What are the boy and girl doing?	The boy and girl are (verb) ing.
Are the girl and boy (verb) ing?	Yes, the girl and boy are (verb) ing.
Are the boy and girl (verb) ing?	No, the boy and girl are not (verb) ing.†
What are the girl and boy doing?	The girl and boy are (verb) ing the (noun).
Are the boy and girl (verb) ing the (noun)?	Yes, the boy and girl are (verb) ing the (noun).
Are the girl and boy (verb) ing the (noun)?	No, the girl and boy are not (verb) ing the (noun).†

*Note. A variety of nouns and verbs should be used.

†Note. Contracted forms should be introduced in beginning primary grades.

TABLE 6.9
Beginning Sentence Patterns—Past Tense*

Question	Answer
What did you have?	I had the (noun).
Did you have the (noun)?	Yes, I had the (noun).
What did you see?	I saw a/an (noun).
Did you see a/an (noun)?	Yes, I saw a/an (noun).
What was the girl/boy doing?	The girl/boy was (verb) ing.
Was the boy/girl (verb) ing?	Yes, the boy/girl was (verb) ing.
What was the girl/boy doing?	The girl/boy was (verb) ing the (noun).
Was the boy/girl (verb) ing the (noun)?	Yes, the boy/girl was (verb) ing the (noun).

*Note. A variety of nouns and verbs should be used.

TABLE 6.10
Past Tense Negatives and Past Tense Plurals*

Question	Answer
Did you have the (noun)?	No, I did not have the (noun).†
Did you see a/an (noun)?	No, I did not see a/an (noun).†
Was the boy/girl (verb) ing?	No, the boy/girl was not (verb) ing.†
Was the girl/boy (verb) ing the (noun)?	No, the girl/boy was not (verb) ing the (noun).†
Did you have the/some (noun) s?	No, I did not have the/some (noun) s.†
Were the boys/girls (verb) ing?	No, the boys/girls were not (verb) ing.†
Were the girls/boys (verb) ing the (noun)?	No, the girls/boys were not (verb) ing the (noun).†

*Note. A variety of nouns and verbs should be used.

†Note. Contracted forms should be introduced in beginning primary grades.

TABLE 6.11
Future Forms*

Question	Answer
What will you do?	I will (<u>verb</u>).
Will you (<u>verb</u>)?	Yes, I will (<u>verb</u>).
Will you (<u>verb</u>)?	No, I will not (<u>verb</u>).†
What will you do?	I will (<u>verb</u>) the (<u>noun</u>).
Will you (<u>verb</u>) the (<u>noun</u>)?	Yes, I will (<u>verb</u>) the (<u>noun</u>).
Will you (<u>verb</u>) the (<u>noun</u>)?	No, I will not (<u>verb</u>) the (<u>noun</u>).†

*Note. A variety of nouns and verbs should be used.

†Note. Contracted forms should be introduced in beginning primary grades.

TABLE 6.12
Compound Subject—Past Tense*

Question	Answer
What were the girl and boy doing?	The girl and boy were (<u>verb</u>) ing.
Were the boy and girl (<u>verb</u>) ing?	Yes, the boy and girl were (<u>verb</u>) ing.
Were the girl and boy (<u>verb</u>) ing?	No, the girl and boy were not (<u>verb</u>) ing.†
What were the boy and girl doing?	The boy and girl were (<u>verb</u>) ing the (<u>noun</u>).
Were the girl and boy (<u>verb</u>) ing the (<u>noun</u>)?	Yes, the girl and boy were (<u>verb</u>) ing the (<u>noun</u>).
Were the boy and girl (<u>verb</u>) ing the (<u>noun</u>)?	No, the boy and girl were not (<u>verb</u>) ing the (<u>noun</u>).†

*Note. A variety of nouns and verbs should be used.

†Note. Contracted forms should be introduced in beginning primary grades.

TABLE 6.13
Compound Subject—Future Form*

Question	Answer
What will the boy and girl do?	The boy and girl will (verb).
Will the girl and boy (verb)?	Yes, the girl and boy will (verb).
Will the boy and girl (verb)?	No, the boy and girl will not (verb).†
What will the girl and boy do?	The girl and boy will (verb) the (noun).
Will the boy and girl (verb) the (verb)?	Yes, the boy and girl will (verb) the (noun).
Will the girl and boy (verb) the (noun)?	No, the girl and boy will not (verb) the (noun).†

*Note. A variety of nouns and verbs should be used.

†Note. Contracted forms should be introduced in beginning primary grades.

TABLE 6.14
Compound Object—Present Tense and Past Tense*

Question	Answer
What do you have?	I have the (noun) and the (noun).
Do you have the (noun) and the (noun)?	Yes, I have the (noun) and the (noun).
Do you have the (noun) and the (noun)?	No, I do not have the (noun) and the (noun).†
What did you have?	I had the (noun) and the (noun).
Did you have the (noun) and the (noun)?	Yes, I had the (noun) and the (noun).
Did you have the (noun) and the (noun)?	No, I did not have the (noun) and the (noun).†

*Note. A variety of nouns should be used.

†Note. Contracted forms should be introduced in beginning primary grades.

TABLE 6.15
Pronouns—Present Tense*

Question	Answer
What do I have?	You have the (noun).
Do I have the (noun)?	Yes, you have the (noun).
Do I have the (noun)?	No, you do not have the (noun).†
What does he/she/it have?	He/she/it has the (noun).
Does he/she/it have the (noun)?	Yes, he/she/it has the (noun).
Does he/she/it have the (noun)?	No, he/she/it does not have the (noun).†
What do we have?	We have the (noun).
Do we have the (noun)?	Yes, we have the (noun).
Do we have the (noun)?	No, we do not have the (noun).†
What do they have?	They have the (noun).
Do they have the (noun)?	Yes, they have the (noun).
Do they have the (noun)?	No, they do not have the (noun).†

*Note. A variety of nouns should be used.

†Note. Contracted forms should be introduced in beginning primary grades.

TABLE 6.16
Pronouns—Past Tense

Question	Answer
What did I have?	You had the (noun).
Did I have the (noun)?	Yes, you had the (noun).
Did I have the (noun) ?	No, you did not have the (noun).†
What did she/he/it have?	She/he/it had the (noun).
Did she/he/it have the (noun)?	Yes, she/he/it had the (noun).

TABLE 6.16 (*cont.*)
Pronouns—Past Tense

Question	Answer
Did she/he/it have the (noun)?	No, she/he/it did not have the (noun).†
What did we have?	We had the (noun).
Did we have the (noun)?	Yes, we had the (noun).
Did we have the (noun)?	No, we did not have the (noun).†
What did they have?	They had the (noun).
Did they have the (noun)?	Yes, they had the (noun).
Did they have the (noun)?	No, they did not have the (noun).†

*Note. A variety of nouns should be used.
†Note. Contracted forms should be introduced in beginning primary grades.

TABLE 6.17
Immediate Future*

Question	Answer
What are you going to do?	I am going to (verb).
Are you going to (verb)?	Yes, I am going to (verb).
Are you going to (verb)?	No, I am not going to (verb).†
What are you going to do?	I am going to (verb) the (noun).
Are you going to (verb) the (noun)?	Yes, I am going to (verb) the (noun).
Are you going to (verb) the (noun)?	No, I am not going to (verb) the (noun).†

*Note. A variety of nouns and verbs should be used.

†Note. Contracted forms should be introduced in beginning primary grades.

PART 4

Activities Related
to the Language
Curriculum

Auditory Training

Importance and Description

Auditory training lessons should teach the hearing-impaired child to make the best use of his residual or remaining hearing. Each hearing-impaired student should have the opportunity to realize his full potential for processing receptive communication information, learning to use and coordinate both vision and residual hearing. Under optimum conditions, the hearing-impaired child will make maximum use of both visual and auditory channels in decoding information. However, specific training in the use of each channel should be done separately to increase skills particular to each channel. In this way, the hearing-impaired child uses his vision and residual hearing with better ability as he uses them together in practical situations.

Regardless of the extent of hearing loss, each child should be given the opportunity to develop as much skill as possible in using residual hearing. The teacher must be careful not to limit the child's opportunities by making inflexible predictions about his auditory abilities based on his audiogram. Each child's potential can only be discovered by experimentation with a variety of auditory tasks; even the most profoundly hearing-impaired child is able to accomplish some auditory tasks. Examples of these tasks include: (a) discrimination and identification of safety sounds, such as traffic noises and fire alarms; and (b) activities involving gross sounds, such as sounds of drum, piano, or horn. The teacher's responsibility is to conduct an individual auditory training program for each child that promotes a positive listening attitude and improves auditory responses to the environment.

Component Skills and Their Order

An auditory training program should include at least four basic categories of tasks: 1) awareness; 2) sound discrimination; 3) speech discrimination; and 4) fine speech discrimination.

Awareness

In awareness, or *on/off* tasks, children must respond to the presence or absence of sound. In a typical awareness lesson, the teacher has a sound maker that he has shown the child. The child has been taught to make a particular response when and only when she hears that sound. Thorough work in awareness tasks is appropriate for preschoolers or children not experienced in auditory training. Sound awareness is a prerequisite skill for any of the more complex discrimination tasks.

One possible awareness or *on/off* lesson goes as follows. The teacher wants the child to raise her hand only when she hears the sound of the drum. To begin, the teacher, with the child facing him, hits the drum and models the desired response (raising hand). Then he hits the drum again, and indicates that it is the child's turn to raise his hand. The teacher can physically assist any child who is still confused. When the child consistently raises her hand each time the teacher hits the drum, she is ready to try the task with her back to the teacher. Now the child must raise her hand each time she hears the sound of the drum, without the visual cue of seeing the teacher. If the child has difficulty at this stage, the teacher may again assist her in raising her hand. Then she should be allowed to try the task again independently. The teacher may continue the physical cue, if necessary, until the child can accomplish the task by herself.

These procedural steps could apply to any awareness task. The two basic components, a sound the teacher makes, and a response to that sound by the child, are always included. However, specific sounds and responses by the child can be varied. Different sound sources might include a record player, tape recorder, piano, bell, horn, clap, and voice. To vary the child's response, the teacher could ask her, each time she hears a sound, to put a peg in a pegboard, put a block in a box, or say the word "on." However, the most straightforward response is that the child simply raises her hand.

The child should also be taught the complementary response, how to indicate *off*. In general, the child's task is to say and sign *off* when a sound stops. This may also involve the child's simultaneously stopping a motion. One possible approach is for the teacher to play music on the record player, teaching the child to walk to the music. When the music begins, the child begins walking, and says and signs *on*. When the music stops, the child must then stop walking, and say and sign *off*. Other variations are possible, including those without physical movement, when the child's only response is to say *off* when a sound stops.

Sound discrimination

In sound discrimination tasks, children must learn a specific response, depending on the particular auditory training unit, and accomplish this response with a variety of sounds. Some examples of sound discrimination tasks involve discriminating: (a) gross noise-maker sounds; (b) fast versus slow rhythms; (c) loud versus quiet sounds; (d) high versus low pitches; and (e) a variety of common environmental sounds.

In a typical sound discrimination lesson, the teacher first familiarizes the child with the task while the child is facing her. An auditory training unit on loud versus quiet sounds will be used as an example. To start, the teacher shows the child the responses that will be expected following either a loud or quiet sound. The most straightforward response would be for the child to simply say and sign *loud* after a loud sound, and *quiet* after a quiet sound. To familiarize young children or auditorally inexperienced children with the expected responses, the teacher could start by modelling correct responses, indicating what the child should imitate. For example, the teacher might play a sound directly on the piano and then say and sign *quiet*. She would then play the quiet sound again and indicate to the child to say and sign *quiet*. This would be repeated until the child consistently and independently said and signed *quiet* at the appropriate time. This sequence would then be repeated with a loud sound on the piano. Next, with the child watching, the teacher would make loud and quiet sounds on each of the sound sources to be used in the unit, and require that the child say and sign either *loud* or *quiet* following each one. Since the child has already learned the correct responses on the first sound source, the piano, he would probably be able to transfer these responses to other sound sources with much less teacher modelling. If the child makes an error, the teacher should correct by modelling the right response, having the child imitate it, and then re-presenting the stimulus, expecting an independent, correct response.

For older children or those familiar with the specific auditory task, the teacher might be able to explain the required response before beginning the lesson. For example, she might tell the child to say and sign *loud* after a loud sound, and *quiet* after a quiet sound. This may be the only explanation necessary. If correction procedures are needed, they would be the same as those used with younger children.

After the child demonstrates his understanding of the specific auditory task by correctly responding while facing the teacher, he must then accomplish the same task with his back to the teacher, using only auditory cues. Procedures for the task, including corrections, are unchanged. The only difference is that now the child is required to discriminate target sounds with his back to the teacher.

Speech discrimination

In speech discrimination tasks, children must learn a specific response, depending on the particular auditory training unit, and generalize this response to a variety of vocalizations, including pitch sounds, directions, inflectional patterns, and words that are sung. Typical speech discrimination tasks could involve discriminating: (a) high versus low pitch sounds; (b) spoken versus sung speech; (c) differences in voices of people; and (d) two-step directions.

The same steps that were described in detail for a typical sound discrimination lesson apply to a typical speech discrimination lesson. Outlined, these steps are: (a) familiarize the child with the task, including the expected response; (b) let the child accomplish the task while facing the sound source; and (c) have the child demonstrate mastery of the task with his back to the sound source. For a more detailed description of these steps, refer to the example of the loud versus quiet sound discrimination task described in the preceding section. A specific auditory training unit for speech discrimination could be substituted within the same format.

Fine speech discrimination

Fine speech discrimination tasks are similar to speech discrimination tasks, except that more subtle discriminations are required. Tasks in this category involve discriminating individual phonemes and words in a variety of auditory training lessons.

The same steps described in detail for a typical sound discrimination lesson and outlined for a typical speech discrimination lesson also apply to fine speech discrimination lessons.

Later in this chapter you will find a more complete list of sound discrimination, speech discrimination, and fine speech discrimination tasks. They are organized in a suggested teaching order, and applicable instructional techniques are included.

Sequenced Auditory Training Curriculum

Introduction

The following tables contain a proposed auditory training curriculum with units organized into four categories: 1) awareness tasks, 2) sound discrimination tasks, 3) speech discrimination tasks, and 4) fine speech discrimination tasks. For units of the latter three categories, teacher action, child response, and suggested sound stimuli are described. In applying the following curriculum, the teacher should require a child's mastery of the awareness tasks as a prerequisite to units of the other three categories. These latter three categories can then be taught parallel to one another, going from the simplest to most complex tasks in each category. A summary of the component units of each of the three categories is given on page 108.

Format

To teach any unit, the teacher must follow two procedural formats. The first format, comprised of three sequenced mastery steps, is detailed in the *loud versus quiet* auditory training unit found in the section on sound discrimination earlier in this chapter. The three ordered mastery steps are:

1. Familiarize the child with the task by telling her what is expected or by modelling the correct response.
2. Have the child independently accomplish the task while facing the sound source, indicating an understanding of the expected response.
3. Have the child demonstrate mastery of the task with her back to the sound source.

The teacher needs this three-step sequence to interpret learner behavior. The purpose of the first two steps is to teach the child the

TABLE 7.1

Summary Table of Auditory Training Units

Sound Discrimination Tasks	Speech Discrimination Tasks	Fine Speech Discrimination Tasks
I. Gross sound discrimination using common noisemakers	I. Discrimination of simple one-part directions	I. Discrimination of mastered vocabulary words in carrier sentences
II. Discrimination of fast versus slow rhythms	II. Discrimination of two-part directions	II. Discrimination of mastered vocabulary words in isolation
III. Discrimination of loud versus quiet sounds	III. Discrimination of high versus low, voiced pitch sounds	III. Discrimination of individual phonetic elements
IV. Discrimination and counting of beats	IV. Discrimination of spoken versus sung speech	IV. Discrimination of individual phonetic sounds and matching them to alphabet letters
V. Auditory-Sequential memory	V. Discrimination of people's voices	V. Discrimination of phonetic elements within words
VI. Discrimination of long versus short sounds	VI. Discrimination of inflectional patterns for statements, questions and exclamations	VI. Discrimination of words differing by one phonetic element, including rhyming words
VII. Discrimination of high versus low pitch sounds	VII. Discrimination of rhythmic phrasing within speech patterns	
VIII. Auditory-sequential memory for high versus low pitch sounds		
IX. Discrimination of common safety sounds		
X. Discrimination of common household sounds		
XI. Discrimination of common human sounds		
XII. Discrimination of common animals sounds		
XIII. Discrimination of common transportation sounds		
XIV. Localization of sounds		

task; any errors she makes indicate her lack of understanding of the task. The teacher can then appropriately correct errors by further explanation or modelling. After the child's understanding has been established in steps 1 and 2, the teacher can use step 3 to find out which sound sources the child can perceive and discriminate in accomplishing the particular task. Now any error the child makes indicates an inability to hear or discriminate a particular sound source, thus giving the teacher useful and specific information about the child's auditory functioning in relation to her hearing loss. Without this three-step process, the teacher would have no way of sorting out errors caused by confusion with the task and errors caused by difficulties with auditory discrimination.

The second format deals with presence and absence of background noise. When children are initially learning and mastering an auditory unit, there should be no distracting noise in the background. After the child has demonstrated mastery of the auditory task, background noise can be introduced, and with each background noise, the child should again be asked to demonstrate mastery of the task. The teacher could choose two or three common noises to use on a regular basis. For example, he might choose tape recordings of music or voices. Again, this step-by-step process allows the teacher to interpret learner behavior. During the first step, when there is no background noise, the teacher identifies the child's auditory functioning in relation to her hearing loss. He can pinpoint and correct errors caused by confusion with the task. The teacher also determines which sound sources the child simply cannot hear or discriminate. In succeeding steps, when background noises are introduced one by one, the teacher can attribute further errors to confusion caused by the particular background noise used.

Two additional effective teaching techniques should be used in applying the sequenced auditory training curriculum. These are:

1. When presenting any sounds for the child to discriminate, start with two that are quite dissimilar and move in degrees to more similar sounds.

2. Have the child learn concepts and accomplish tasks on one or two sound sources first, then slowly introduce more.

Sequenced auditory training curriculum

The tasks found in the Summary Table of Auditory Training Units are detailed in the following pages. We have suggested a chart format containing target tasks within units and spaces for recording mastery data and comments.

TABLE 7.2
Sound Discrimination Auditory Training

Units*	Start Date	Mastery Date
I. Gross Sound Discrimination Using Common Noisemakers *Objective:* Given a preselected number of common noisemakers, the child will discriminate and name each one (with verbalization and sign) after it is produced by the teacher; 100% accuracy is required for mastery. *Suggested Sound Stimuli:* drum, bell (variety), horn, piano, buzzer board, clapping, voice (spoken words, counting). *Teacher Action:* produces a sound with the target noisemaker (by the end of the unit, all of the common noisemakers selected by the teacher will have been presented). *Child Response:* says and signs the name of the target noisemaker.		
II. Discrimination of Fast Versus Slow Rhythms *Objective:* Given a preselected number of sound sources, the child will discriminate and name a fast or slow rhythm played on each by appropriately saying and signing the words "fast" or "slow"; 100% accuracy is required for mastery. *Suggested Sound Stimuli:* drum, bell, (variety), piano, recorded music, clapping, voice (spoken words, singing, counting). *Teacher Action:* produces a fast or slow rhythm on one of the predetermined sound sources (by the end of the unit, both a fast and slow rhythm will have been played on each of the sound sources selected by the teacher). *Child Response:* says and signs the appropriate word "fast" or "slow" after the rhythm.		

III. **Discrimination Of Loud Versus Quiet Sounds**

Objective: Given a preselected number of sound sources, the child will discriminate and name a loud or quiet sound played on each, by appropriately saying and signing the words "loud" or "quiet"; 100% accuracy is required for mastery.

Suggested Sound Stimuli: drum, bell (variety), piano, recorded music, clapping, voice (speaking, singing).

Teacher Action: produces a loud or quiet sound on one of the predetermined sound sources (by the end of the unit, both a loud and quiet sound will have been played on each of the sound sources selected by the teacher).

Child Response: says and signs the appropriate word "loud" or "quiet" after the sound.

IV. **Discrimination And Counting Of Beats**

Objective: Given a preselected number of sound sources, the child will discriminate and count the number of beats played on each, by saying and signing the correct number of beats played (appropriately corresponding to counting ability of individual children, with number of beats ranging from 0-21); 100% accuracy is required for mastery.

Suggested Sound Stimuli: drum, bell (variety), piano, clapping, voice (repetition of one word).

Teacher Action: produces the predetermined number of beats on one of the sound sources (by the end of the unit, all of the sound sources selected by the teacher will have been used for the range of beats appropriate to the child's counting ability).

Child Response: says and signs the correct number word corresponding to the number of beats played.

V. **Auditory-Sequential Memory**

Objective: Given a preselected number of sound sources, the child will discriminate a predetermined number of sounds in a series (ranging from 3 to 5, and appropriate to the child's age and ability level), and name (say and sign) those sounds in the order in which they were made; 80% accuracy is required for mastery.

TABLE 7.2 (cont.)
Sound Discrimination Auditory Training

Units*	Start Date	Mastery Date
Suggested Sound Stimuli: drum, bell (variety), horn, piano, clapping, voice (words and speech sounds).		
Teacher Action: produces a series of sounds on the predetermined sound sources (by the end of the unit, all the sound sources selected by the teacher will have been used in various combinations, including repetitions of sounds within a series).		
Child Response: says and signs the names of the sound sources in the order in which they were played.		
VI. **Discrimination Of Long Versus Short Sounds**		
Objective: Given a preselected number of sound sources, the child will discriminate and name a long or short sound played on each by appropriately saying and signing the words "long" or "short"; 100% accuracy is required for mastery.		
Suggested Sound Stimuli: tone bell, horn, piano, buzzer board, voice (spoken or sung vowels).		
Teacher Action: produces a long or short sound on one of the predetermined sound sources (by the end of the unit, both a long and short sound will have been played on each of the sound sources selected by the teacher).		
Child Response: says and signs the appropriate word "long" or "short" after the sound.		
VII. **Auditory-Sequential Memory For Long Versus Short Sounds**		
Objective: Given a preselected number of sound sources, the child will discriminate a series of long and short sounds played on *only one sound source* (ranging from 2 to 15 long and short sounds, and appropriate to the child's age and ability level), and name those sounds in the order in which they were played; 80% accuracy is required for mastery.		

Suggested Sound Stimuli: tone bell, horn, piano, buzzer board, voice (spoken and sung speech).

Teacher Action: produces a series of long and short sounds on one predetermined sound source (by the end of the unit, all of the sound sources selected by the teacher will have been used).

Child Response: says and signs the words "long" and "short" in the order in which they were played.

VIII. **Discrimination Of High Versus Low Pitch Sounds**

Objective: Given a preselected number of sound sources, the child will discriminate and name a high or low sound played on each, by appropriately saying and signing the words "high" or "low"; 100% accuracy is required for mastery.

Suggested Sound Stimuli: tone bells, xylophone, piano, musical instruments (variety), voice (spoken and sung words).

Teacher Action: produces a high or low sound on one of the preselected sound sources (by the end of the unit, both a high and low sound will have been played on each of the sound sources selected by the teacher).

Child Response: says and signs the appropriate word "high" or "low" after the sound.

IX. **Auditory-Sequential Memory For High Versus Low Sounds**

Objective: Given a preselected number of sound sources, the child will discriminate a series of high and low sounds played on *only one sound source* (ranging from 2 to 5 high and low sounds, and appropriate to the child's age and ability level), and name those sounds in the order in which they were played; 80% accuracy is required for mastery.

Suggested Sound Stimuli: tone bells, xylophone, piano, musical instruments (variety), voice (spoken and sung words).

Teacher Action: produces a series of high and low sounds on one predetermined sound source (by the end of the unit, all of the sound sources selected by the teacher will have been used).

Child Response: says and signs the words "high" and "low" in the order in which they were played.

TABLE 7.2 (cont.)
Sound Discrimination Auditory Training

Units*	Start Date	Mastery Date
X. Discrimination Of Common Safety Sounds *Objective:* Given a preselected number of common safety sounds, the child will discriminate and name each one (with verbalization and sign) after it is produced by the teacher; 100% accuracy is required for mastery. *Suggested Sound Stimuli:* (the following sounds are presented on tape or a record, or, when possible, by the real sound source): sirens (ambulance, fire engine), horn honking, car engine, voice (commands such as "stop," "look out," "watch out," "be careful"). *Teacher Action:* produces a target safety sound (by the end of the unit, all of the safety sounds selected by the teacher will have been presented). *Child Response:* says and signs the name of the target safety sound. **XI. Discrimination Of Common Household Sounds** *Objective:* Given a preselected number of common household sounds, the child will discriminate and name each one (with verbalization and sign) after it is produced by the teacher; 100% accuracy is required for mastery. *Suggested Sound Stimuli:*** (presented on tape or record, or, when possible, by the real sound source): door closing, door bell, knocking, telephone, vacuum cleaner, typewriter, toilet flushing, alarm clock. *Teacher Action:* produces a target household sound (by the end of the unit, all of the household sounds selected by the teacher will have been presented). *Child Response:* says and signs the name of the target household sound.		

XII. **Discrimination Of Common Human Sounds**

Objective: Given a preselected number of common human sounds, the child will discriminate and name each one (with verbalization and sign) after it is produced by the teacher; 100% accuracy is required for mastery.

Suggested Sound Stimuli:** (presented on tape or record, or, when possible, by the real sound source): laughing, coughing, sneezing, crying, snoring, talking, singing, whistling.

Teacher Action: produces a target human sound (by the end of the unit, all of the human sounds selected by the teacher will have been presented).

Child Response: says and signs the name of the target human sound.

XIII. **Discrimination Of Common Animal Sounds**

Objective: Given a preselected number of common animal sounds, the child will discriminate and name each one (with verbalization and sign) after it is produced by the teacher; 100% accuracy is required for mastery.

Suggested Sound Stimuli:** (presented on tape or record, or, when possible, by the real sound source): cow, dog, cat, pig, duck, sheep, chicken, horse, owl, lion.

Teacher Action: produces a target animal sound (by the end of the unit, all of the animal sounds selected by the teacher will have been presented).

Child Response: says and signs the name of the target animal.

XIV. **Discrimination Of Common Transportation Sounds.**

Objective: Given a preselected number of common transportation sounds, the child will discriminate and name each one (with verbalization and sign), after it is produced by the teacher; 100% accuracy is required for mastery.

Suggested Sound Stimuli: (presented on tape or record, or, when possible, by the real sound source): airplane, train (whistle), motor vehicles, boat (horn), helicopter.

Teacher Action: produces a target transportation sound (by the end of the unit, all of the transportation sounds selected by the teacher will have been presented).

Child Response: says and signs the name of the target transportation sound.

TABLE 7.2 (cont.)
Sound Discrimination Auditory Training

Units*	Start Date	Mastery Date
XV. Localization Of Sounds *Objective:* Given a preselected number of sound sources, the child will localize and identify, by pointing or naming, the position of the sound just produced by the teacher (with a finite set of possible positions having been told to the child): 80% accuracy is required for mastery. *Suggested Sound Stimuli:* drum, bell (variety), horn, clapping, voice (child's own name, words, sentences). *Suggested Places For Teacher to Stand:* to the right, left, front, and back of the child. *Teacher Action:* produces a sound on one sound source while standing in one of the possible positions. *Child Response:* indicates where the sound has been produced, by pointing or naming the teacher's position (with words such as "right," "left," "in front," "in back").		

---

*Note. These units are to be taught parallel to the speech discrimination and fine speech discrimination auditory training units. Suggested sound stimuli provide a selection from which to choose. In any unit, one or two sound sources should be presented initially, as the child is learning the task. Other sound sources are added as the child demonstrates mastery of each preceding sound source. Extra space in the "Start Date" and "Mastery Date" columns can be used for comments when needed.

**Note. Tape recordings and records of these sounds may be commercially available.

TABLE 7.5
Speech Discrimination Auditory Training

Units*	Start Date	Mastery Date

I. Discrimination Of Simple One-Part Directions

Objective: Given a preselected number of simple, one-part directions, the child will discriminate and follow each direction after it has been said and signed by the teacher; 100% accuracy is required for mastery.

Suggested Directions: "Stand up," "Sit down," "Get your coat," "Clap your hands," "Walk to the wall," "Jump," "Turn Around."

Teacher Action: says and signs one of the target one-part directions.

Child Response: correctly follows the target one-part direction.

II. Discrimination of Two-Part Directions

Objective: Given a preselected number of two-part directions, the child will discriminate and follow each direction after it has been said and signed by the teacher; 100% accuracy is required for mastery.

Suggested Directions: Many combinations of two simple one-part directions are possible; for example, "Get your coat, and walk to your desk," or "Walk around the table, and write your name on the chalk board."

Teacher Action: says and signs one of the target two-part directions.

Child Response: correctly follows the target two-part direction.

III. Discrimination Of High Versus Low, Voiced Pitch Sounds

Objective: The child will discriminate and name a high or low sound, either spoken or sung by the teacher, by appropriately saying and signing the words "high" or "low"; 100% accuracy is required for mastery.

Suggested Voice Stimuli: spoken and sung words and vowels.

Teacher Action: speaks or sings a high- or low-pitched sound.

Child Response: says and signs the appropriate word "high" or "low" after the spoken or sung pitch sound.

TABLE 7.3 (cont.)
Speech Discrimination Auditory Training

Units*	Start Date	Mastery Date
IV. Discrimination Of Spoken Versus Sung Speech *Objective*: The child will discriminate and name spoken or sung phrases and sentences by appropriately saying and signing the words "talking" or "singing"; 100% accuracy is required for mastery. *Suggested Spoken and Sung Stimuli*: portions of familiar nursery rhymes and songs, common phrases and sentences. *Teacher Action*: speaks or sings target phrases or sentences. *Child Response*: says and signs "talking" or "singing" after the appropriate spoken or sung stimulus.		
V. Discrimination Of People's Unique Voices *Objective*: Given a preselected number of people's voices, the child will discriminate and name each one (with verbalization and sign) after it is produced by the teacher; 100% accuracy is required for mastery. *Suggested Voice Stimuli*: taped or recorded voices of: adult male, adult female, child saying phrases or sentences, or baby talking baby-talk. *Teacher Action*: produces a target voice sound (by the end of the unit, all of the voice sounds selected by the teacher will have been presented). *Child Response*: names (with verbalization and sign) the target voice just produced.		

VI. **Discrimination Of Inflectional Patterns For Statements, Questions, And Exclamations**

Objective: Given a preselected number of statements, questions, and exclamations, the child will discriminate and imitate each one with the proper voice inflection and signs immediately following its production by the teacher; 100% accuracy is required for mastery.

Suggested Inflectional Patterns: common statements, questions, and exclamations, produced with voice pitch changes appropriate to each.

Teacher Action: produces a target statement, question, or exclamation, using the correct inflectional pattern (by the end of the unit, several examples of each of the target inflectional patterns will have been presented).

Child Response: imitates (says and signs) the target statement, question, or exclamation just produced by the teacher, using the correct inflectional pattern.

VII. **Discrimination Of Rhythmic Phrasing Within Speech Patterns**

Objective: Given a preselected number of sentences which contain two phrases separated by a comma, the child will discriminate and imitate each modelled sentence, pausing between phrases, as indicated by the comma; 100% accuracy is required for mastery.

Suggested Sentence stimuli: common sentences composed of two phrases separated by a comma (number of phrases and commas could be varied after this first sentence type is mastered).

Teacher Action: produces a target sentence, using the correct phrasing (by the end of the unit, a variety of sentences will have been presented).

Child Response: imitates (says and signs) the target sentence just produced by the teacher, using the correct phrasing.

*Note. These units are to be taught parallel to the sound discrimination and fine speech discrimination auditory training units. Suggested speech stimuli provide a selection from which to choose. In any unit, one or two stimuli should be presented initially, as the child is learning the task. Other stimuli are added as the child demonstrates mastery of the preceding stimuli. Extra space in the "Start Date" and "Mastery Date" columns can be used for comments when needed.

119

TABLE 7.4
Fine Speech Discrimination Auditory

Training Units*	Start Date	Mastery Date

I. **Discrimination Of Mastered Vocabulary Words In Carrier Sentences**

Objective: Given a finite set of vocabulary words within one vocabulary unit, the child will discriminate each word in a simple carrier sentence (such as "Touch the _____," or "Point to the _____,"), and perform the correct action; 100% accuracy is required for mastery.

Suggested Fine Speech Stimuli: mastered words within one vocabulary unit per auditory training lesson. Throughout the school year, all vocabulary units can be used.

Teacher Action: says and signs a carrier sentence (direction) containing a target vocabulary word.

Child Response: performs the correct action using the target vocabulary word.

II. **Discrimination Of Mastered Vocabulary Words In Isolation**

Objective: Given a finite set of vocabulary words within one vocabulary unit, the child will discriminate each word and repeat the word, using speech and sign, immediately following its production by the teacher; 100% accuracy is required for mastery.

Suggested Fine Speech Stimuli: mastered words within one vocabulary unit per auditory training lesson. Throughout the school year, all vocabulary units can be used.

Teacher Action: says and signs a target vocabulary word.

Child Response: says and signs the target vocabulary word, immediately following the teacher's production.

III. **Discrimination Of Individual Phonetic Elements**

Objective: Given a preselected number of individual phonetic elements, the child will discriminate and imitate each one immediately following its production by the teacher; 80% accuracy is required for mastery.

Suggested Fine Speech Stimuli: vowel, diphthong, consonant, and blend sounds, in that order.

Teacher Action: says a target phonetic element.

Child Response: imitates the target phonetic element, immediately following the teacher's production.

IV. **Discrimination Of Individual Phonetic Sounds And Matching Them To Alphabet Letters**

Objective: Given a set of cards, each with one printed alphabet letter on it, the child will discriminate the spoken sound that goes with each letter and pick out the corresponding alphabet letter card; 80% accuracy is required for mastery.

Suggested Fine Speech Stimuli: spoken sounds corresponding to the individual alphabet letters.

Teacher Action: says one of the sounds corresponding to an alphabet letter (by the end of the unit, all of the alphabet letters will have been attempted).

Child Response: chooses alphabet letter card responding to the target sound produced by the teacher.

V. **Discrimination Of Phonetic Elements Within Words**

Objective: Given a preselected number of phonetic elements, the child, after being told which one to listen for, will discriminate the target phoneme in a word and tell the teacher if it occurred in the beginning, middle, or final position; 80% accuracy is required for mastery.

Suggested Fine Speech Stimuli: words containing target vowels, diphthongs, consonants and blend sounds in that order.

TABLE 7.4
Fine Speech Discrimination Auditory

Training Units*	Start Date	Mastery Date

Teacher Action: says and signs a word containing the target phonetic element in one of the three positions (initial, medial, final), after informing the child which sound to listen for.

Child Response: says and signs "beginning," "middle," or "end," corresponding to the position of the target phonetic element.

VI. **Discrimination Of Words Differing By One Phonetic Element, Including Rhyming Words**

Objective: Given a preselected number of word pairs differing by one phonetic element, for each pair said and signed by the teacher the child will discriminate the two words, determine if they are the same or different, and then respond in the following way: 1) repeat (say and sign) the two words just produced by the teacher; 2) say and sign "same" or "different"; 80% accuracy is required for mastery

Suggest Fine Speech Stimuli: pairs of one-syllable words; 1) differing by one phonetic element in the initial position (rhyming words), e.g., "man/can"; 2) differing by one vowel sound in the middle position, e.g., "boat/bite"; 3) differing by one vowel ·sound or consonant in the final position, e.g., "day/do," or "line/light."

Teacher Action: says and signs a target word pair.

Child Response: repeats (says and signs) the target word pair, then says and signs the word "same" or "different."

*Note. These units are to be taught parallel to the sound discrimination and speech discrimination auditory training units. Suggested fine speech stimuli provide a selection from which to choose. In any unit, one or two stimuli should be presented initially as the child is learning the task. Other stimuli are added as the child demonstrates mastery of the preceding stimuli. Extra space in the "Start Date" and "Mastery Date" columns can be used for comments when needed.

In applying the sequenced auditory training curriculum, the teacher must remember that the three categories of units should be taught simultaneously (refer to the Summary Table of Auditory Training Units, page 108). Within each category, units were sequenced according to difficulty, with simpler ones listed first and subsequent units becoming more and more complex and subtle. However, in following the suggested order, the teacher must remain flexible because some children will not be able to master particular units. Such children should be allowed to proceed with their classmates in continuing with succeeding tasks in the sequence. The teacher can return them to units not mastered at a later time.

Enrichment Activities

Language Experiences

The goal of any language curriculum for hearing-impaired children must be to foster each child's ability to partake to the fullest extent possible in the culture of his community and to be able to play a role in the formulation and transmittal of that culture. Though most of this book is devoted to assuring that hearing-impaired children acquire vocabulary and English grammar in a structured systematic fashion, we realize that our efforts can be deemed successful only when this language is brought out of the tutoring session or structured classroom and into spontaneous, everyday use by the child. Therefore, all our teaching must be aimed at having the child gain interest and facility in the language he has painstakingly acquired.

Denotative and connotative meaning

Each content word in the English language may be usefully thought of as having two types of meaning. The *denotative* meaning corresponds roughly to the dictionary definition of the word. The denotative meaning can be specified by stating the properties or patterns of stimulation that are critical to its socially approved use. To specify these characteristics one must be able to indicate: (a) what characteristics a thing, event, or property must have in order to be called by that name; and (b) what characteristics a thing, event, or property may have that exclude it from being called by that name. As an illustration, a child who has been taught in a tutoring session to respond to a single picture of an apple by saying and signing *apple*

Language experience charts encourage early English output and reading. The student teacher is conducting a language experience activity with a group of preschool children.

shows that she understands part of the denotative meaning of that word. When she responds to *all* pictures of apples—whether they are small, large, green, red, yellow, cut or peeled—by saying "apple"; when she never says "apple" in response to any other picture—a peach, pear, or tomato—she may be said to know the denotative meaning of *apple*. This illustration is appropriate for concrete nouns, verbs, and other parts of speech that can be depicted by pictures, actions, or real objects.

Other denotative meanings are obviously more complex. *Justice, truth, mercy,* and *love* can not easily be taught through pictures. They generally require verbal explanations as well as verbal examples of critical incidents.

Connotative meaning, on the other hand, is an idiosyncratic response to non-criterial attributes—what the word, and its object, means to the person, as opposed to its dictionary or denotative meaning. Thus, the word *apple* to some children would have myriad associations. They have tasted apples, cut apples, peeled apples, planted apple seeds, baked apples, made applesauce, and in each of these experiences have used the word *apple*. *Apple* for them might have a rich connotative association. Another group of children who have only learned the word through pictures in tutoring sessions may be programmed to give the expected response, but it is unlikely that they will use the word spontaneously and meaningfully in everyday situations; to them, the word is sterile, devoid of positive and negative associations, and thus useless in the real world.

The more connotative associations a word has for a child, the more its meaning for him, and the more likely he is to use it appropriately in everyday life.

Part of the responsibility of teachers of hearing-impaired children is to assure transfer of training from the tutoring session to the everyday world through language experiences. These experiences can be provided in many class activities, including field trips, simulations, demonstrations, creative dramatics, stories, music, dance, pantomime, and art. Table 8.1 lists the language experiences offered to one class of kindergarten/first grade children during one academic year. They are grouped by vocabulary unit.

As can be seen by the activities included in the list on the following page, language experiences can be carefully planned to accompany the vocabulary lessons and contribute positively to the student's cognitive and social development. The following sections briefly discuss each type of language experience activity and guidelines for its appropriate use.

Classroom Activities

Language experience classroom activities should give each student the opportunity to use all applicable senses—audition, taction, gustation, olfaction, and vision—to gain connotative as well as denotative meaning from the vocabulary and concepts being presented. A skilled language experience teacher can turn a mundane activity, such as making muffins or eating a peach, into an individualized, exciting experience for the whole group. New vocabulary is reviewed and reinforced, grammatical forms are practiced, and each child participates at his or her own level.

Each classroom language activity has three phases. In phase one, the teacher introduces the activity, shows and explains the materials to be used, discusses the new vocabulary and concepts, and, making sure she has their interest and attention, asks the children questions. In phase two, the activity is undertaken, with teacher assistance if necessary. Here, much individualization is possible; each child can

TABLE 8.1
Language Experiences Grouped By Vocabulary Unit

Foods

Our lunch (C.A.)
Cornbread muffins (C.A.)
Our popcorn (C.A.)
Banana splits (C.A.)
Shopping for lunch (F.T.)
Pike Place Market (F.T.)
Sweet potatoes (C.A.)
Making the cake (C.A.)
The artichoke (C.A.)
Onions, celery, cauliflower (C.A.)
Orange Jello (C.A.)
The pineapple (C.A.)
Making bread (C.A.)
Vegetable soup (C.A.)
Eating corn (C.A.)
Eating carrots (C.A.)
The berries (C.A.)
The fruitman (D)
Our lemonade (C.D.)
The peach (C.A.)

Making strawberry shortcake (C.A.)
Our peanut butter cookies (C.A.)
The picnic (F.T.)
The animal cookies (C.A.)
The rotten coconut (C.A.)
The honeycomb (C.A.)
Going to the grocery store (F.T.)
Cooking beans and peas (C.A.)
Making ice cream (C.A.)
Making butter (C.A.)
Clam chowder for lunch (C.A.)
Eatin crab (C.A.)
Making cupcakes (C.A.)
Making orange juice (C.A.)
Our fruit basket (C.A.)
The grapes (C.A.)
The watermelon (C.A.)
The cantaloupe (C.A.)
Our gingerbread boys (C.A.)
Making hot chocolate (C.A.)

Holidays and Seasons

Andrew's pumpkin farm (F.T.)
Our jack-o'-lantern (C.A.)
Dying the Easter eggs (A)
Blowing eggs (A)
Spring time (D)
Marshmallow snowmen (A)
Flying a kite (F.T.)

Our spring walk (F.T.)
Eastern bunny puppets (A)
Birthday parties (S)
Marching with flags (C.A.)
Our Santa Claus (D)
Christmas ornaments (A)
Making Christmas stockings (A)
Making a snowman (A)

Health and Safety

Visiting the nurse (C.A.)
The nurse (D)

The dentist (Story)
Keeping well (D)
Our safety walk (F.T.)

Transportation

The ferry trip (F.T.)
The dining car (C.D.)

The mail car (C.A.)
The train trip (F.T.)

be asked to perform that portion of the activity most suited to his physical, cognitive, or language ability. During the activity the teacher and children discuss the tasks at hand. In phase three, after completion of the activity, the teacher and children discuss and recreate the activity by using the children's own language and recording the activity "story" on a chart. They might write captions to photos or drawings, or write individual stories and poems about the activity. Composing a newsletter for family or school friends is another way of recreating the activity. Thus, activity work is once again individualized so that each child can practice the vocabulary and language structures appropriate to his or her level. Writing the story is also an excellent medium for reinforcing spelling, punctuation, handwriting, or typing skills.

Field Trips

Field trips take children away from the classroom and show them things that cannot be adequately recreated in the classroom. Because field trips require money and time allowances, they can only be justified when they contribute positively to a planned curriculum sequence and when their benefits cannot be simulated in the classroom. Unless the teacher is already familiar with the places to be visited, he should visit the site in advance to determine if: (a) the visit will indeed provide the class with the planned experience; (b) the site is accessible to children in wheelchairs or with mobility problems; (c) special arrangements are needed for an interpreter's lighting or physical accommodation; and (d) appropriate preparation is needed, including preparing children for special behavior rules, (e.g., in certain museums, exhibits cannot be touched; at the zoo, certain animals cannot be fed) and for applicable special vocabulary and concepts.

Care must be taken to ensure that the field trip will provide experiences at the right level for the class; it should not be so overwhelming or so crowded that the children cannot focus on the relevant aspects of the experience. For example, if children age 6 through 8 are learning vocabulary words associated with air transportation, a visit to a major metropolitan airport might be too complex for learning such terms as runway, control tower, windsock, takeoff, landing, etc. The sheer size of the airport and the myriad activities going on can overwhelm a child so much that she is unable to benefit from the experiences provided. One early field trip experience well remembered is that of a 12-year-old, who, after spending a day at New York's huge, crowded Museum of Natural History and visiting the Planetarium as well, was asked to draw a picture of something he saw and liked best. Confidently, he drew a fire extinguisher located in a case near the stairs of the museum. In the maze of overwhelming crowds and experiences, that extinguisher was evidently the only thing he could relate to! Field trips for young children should be relatively short, relaxed, and directed by the teacher. A walk down a wooded path, a stroll around the school, or an elevatoɪ ride to a high-rise apartment is often sufficient stimulation for conversation, art projects, and composition. Each trip can also provide an experiential base for later language lessons. As children mature, field trips can become longer and more complex, allowing the students quite a bit of independent exploration.

Like each classroom activity, a field trip has three basic phases. In the preparation phase, the teacher introduces new vocabulary and concepts, discusses the site and purpose of the field trip, and, with student participation lists special rules for field trip behavior. As one outcome of the preparation phase, the teacher assigns each child a specific activity to undertake while on the trip. Each activity focuses the children's attention on those aspects of the experience the teacher considers most important. Activities might include: (a) buying certain items at a grocery store; (b) checking off a list of the different animals seen at the zoo; (c) taking notes on exhibits visited at the museum; or (d) asking specific questions during a tour. It is often a good idea for the teacher to take still or moving pictures or videotape children's experiences during the field trip. In phase 3, after the trip and in subsequent language classes, the teacher uses procedures similar to those used for classroom experiences to record the field trip in permanent form. Like the permanent records of classroom activities, the field trip records are taken out and reviewed periodically for vocabulary and concept recall; they can also be used to teach the relevant expressions such as: at Christmas time, three months ago, last year, and in April.

Creative Dramatics and Simulations

Some of the most potent learning tools a teacher can use to help develop children's language and stimulate their independent thinking are creative dramatics and simulation activities. When used in the classroom, creative dramatics allow the child to actively participate in situations, and practice language, social, and cognitive skills in a sheltered environment. At more advanced levels, creative dramatics allow the student to recreate fictional, historical, or current events through role playing, and help him gain new insight into the nature of events. Table 8.2 depicts some of the many ways in which creative dramatics can be useful.

TABLE 8.2
Creative Dramatics

Elementary Level
Recreating stories from reading books
Acting out fairy tales
Depicting events that will happen to a child in the group
    a trip to the hospital
    a family wedding
    a plane trip
    a new baby in the family
Depicting events in which the group will participate
    practicing for a field trip
    greeting visitors
    being hosts at a party for parents
Recreating events which allow the children to discover alternative solutions
    classroom fights
    misbehavior
    inappropriate social reactions

Secondary Level
Recreating historical events or conditions
    the beginning of World War I (assassination of Archduke Ferdinand)
    the industrial revolution
    women's suffrage movement
Simulating anticipated personal experiences
    job interviews
    driver's examination
    renting an apartment
    buying a house
    getting a traffic ticket
    appearing in court

Note. Some of these experiences for some of the students will involve using an interpreter; specific training and simulation in using a medical or legal interpreter should be given.

"True" creative dramatics

Writing, producing, directing, and/or acting in a stage show can be based after the models provided by National Theatre of the Deaf.

Creative dramatics involves four phases: preparation, rehearsal, performance, and discussion. In the first phase, preparation, actors are assigned their roles, based on a discussion of the topic to be dramatized. The teacher and the students prepare a script or script outline. Older children discuss the vocabulary and concepts, as well as the alternate ways of expressing them in dramatic form. Young children or less advanced students usually memorize a script *per se.* Others might ad lib from a script outline prepared with room for imagination. Simple props can be constructed from readily available materials. For young students, simple costume parts (e.g., ears to represent a rabbit; white coat to represent a nurse, doctor, or dentist) often remind them of their assumed roles. For older students, small name tags remind them of their more complex roles (e.g., tenement owner, landlady, unemployed miner,). All this preparation takes varying amounts of time, from a day for young children and simple situations, to several weeks for older children and complex situations. Rehearsal of the script in its entirety takes place in the second phase. The script can be refined, and speech and sign production can be corrected. Rehearsal can often be eliminated if the preceding preparation has been thorough. In the third phase the actual performance is given, perhaps once sans audience, or several times for classmates, normal peers, parents, or community groups. In the last phase, the class discusses the performance and records it in permanent form as a language experience story.

A special type of language experience is essential for preparing hearing-impaired children to cope with the real world. This special language experience is practice communication with people who are naive about deafness, deaf speech, and sign language. Children taught in an environment where Total Communication is used both at home and at school, and where the student communication attempts are understood, often cannot cope adequately when trying to communicate with hearing people such as policemen, shopkeepers, service providers, or bureaucrats. Based on his abilities in speech and lipreading, each child should practice speaking, lipreading, and/or writing short notes to convey and obtain specific information. This skill must be practiced in realistic situations where the hearing people involved, though providing a permissive atmosphere for practice, are genuinely unable to communicate via sign.

At young ages, children should be encouraged to convey messages or obtain information from school personnel using notes or speech patterns prepared in class. As their sophistication increases, students can be given assignments to obtain specific information from out-of-school personnel such as city or county officials, community helpers, or prospective employers. In preparation for these assignments, sample scripts might be practiced in school, using simulation techniques.

Reading and Writing Captions

New technology now provides the deaf population with ways of receiving information from the visual media of television and film. By *open captioning* (i.e., captions visible to every viewer, as are captions in foreign films) deaf people get an abbreviated version of screen dialogue, or have access of off-camera narrative. A new technological development, called *closed captioning*, will greatly increase the availability of captions to deaf people. Under this system, captions are shown under many commercial and public television programs. While these captions will not be available to the general population they will be available to those whose television sets are equipped with special decoders. Thus, hearing-impaired people will find the information they need, and hearing viewers will not be distracted by extraneous captions.

While captioning, especially closed captioning will open up new vistas for the hearing impaired, it also reveals some new educational needs. Most deaf children have far fewer reading vocabulary and comprehension skills than their hearing peers. Reading captions can be considered an extremely specialized form of reading; it differs from reading print material in several important ways.

1. Captioned material is more condensed than most other written material. The amount of novel content is often very high. Because of space and time limitations, few extraneous words are used.

2. Captioned material is presented temporally. As one word (or one set of captions) disappears, another takes its place. The reader has no opportunity to go back and review past material in reference to new information; he cannot reread a caption. Furthermore, captions demand that the reader keep a steady reading pace over a long period of time. They require reading fluency and enough flexibility to move easily to the next caption, perhaps without a full understanding of the previous one; this calls for a relatively long attention span.

3. Captions of most movies and TV shows, other than news shows and documentaries, contain an extremely high proportion of dialogue. Personal pronouns are used frequently, while their referents change constantly. To understand these captions and, indeed, most captioned material, the reader must simultaneously extract meaning from the picture and the caption, using one to help interpret the other.

Thus, all reading programs for hearing-impaired children should contain specific instruction in the skills essential for reading captions. These skills are:

1. An understanding of visual stimuli, such as movies and television programs.
2. Reading at a steady pace over a long period (e.g., ½ hour) with few or no breaks.
3. Comprehension of material without reference to previously covered text.
4. Comprehension of dialogue.

For instructional purposes, captioned materials such as filmstrips and movies should be shown regularly in the classroom. The teacher should emphasize that children obtain information from the captions. Children should also be given the opportunity to write captions for commercial or homemade movies or TV programs. Lowenbraun and Scroggs (1974) describe an easy method for writing and displaying captions to accompany a commercially available movie or filmstrip. Hearing-impaired children should practice watching an interpreter as they simultaneously gain information from visual mediums such as films or TV.

Using the teletypewriter

Another recent technological innovation that opens new horizons for deaf individuals and simultaneously poses a challenge to language instruction is the teletypewriter (TTY). A TTY can be hooked up to a telephone and enables a deaf person to transmit messages, via a written form, by typing them. The typewritten messages are then received by another TTY unit at the other end of the telephone line.

Music, Rhythms, and Dance

A music, rhythms, and dance curriculum is valuable to hearing-impaired children. The teacher uses each aspect of the curriculum to teach specific skills or to increase children's specific capabilities. The curriculum should include:

Music Section (Use of songs)
  1. Ability to sing and sign the lyrics to a variety of songs (children's songs, holiday songs, contemporary songs).

2. Increased awareness of speech sounds within song lyrics and more precise articulation of these sounds.

3. Increased ability to discriminate recorded words, for children who are auditorially capable.

4. Increased ability for rhythmic signing through flowing movement to music.

Dance Section (Use of recorded dance music)
1. Increased coordination (large motor) abilities through varied dance movements.

2. Increased awareness of and ability to perform various dances and dance steps.

3. Increased ability to move rhythmically to recorded dance music.

A music, rhythms, and dance program gives hearing-impaired children the chance to develop coordination and music skills. Maria and Stephen are taking their turn in the Virginia Reel.

4. Increased ability to discriminate recorded sounds and/or to feel the vibrations of those sounds, for children who are auditorally capable.

Rhythms Section (Use of a perceptual motor program: see Table 10.12 and accompanying explanation)

In addition to the rhythmic skills developed as part of the music and dance sections:

1. Increased ability to read a series of rhythmic symbols on cards in a left-to-right reading progression.

2. Increased ability to follow different rhythmic patterns with correct *movement* or *rest* performances.

3. Increased ability to use appropriate rhythm instruments and voices in varied rhythmic patterns.

Hearing children have frequent opportunities to learn the skills listed above, but hearing-impaired children do not acquire them on their own. Therefore, such a curriculum has to be planned and built into the general school curriculum. The following is one possible approach.

A half-hour block of time could be planned into the daily schedule for music, rhythms, and dance activities. Two days per week could be assigned for songs, 2 days for dance, and 1 day for rhythms. For the rhythms section, the teacher can use a commercially available perceptual motor program. It gives each child the opportunity to perform a variety of rhythmic patterns, as shown by graphics indicating particular movements or rests. Mastery data should be posted on a chart, as a child's mastery of one pattern is a prerequisite for moving to the next.

The following steps are used to teach songs on music days.

Step 1   A chart with printed lyrics of each song is prepared.

Step 2   The teacher presents a song to the children by saying and signing each word on the chart. Words the children might not understand are explained at this time.

Step 3   The children as a group practice saying and signing the lyrics with the teacher.

Step 4   The teacher sings and signs the song for the children, with accompanying record or musical instrument, if available.

Step 5   The children as a group practice singing and signing the lyrics with the teacher. Steps 1 through 5 are all covered on the day a song is introduced.

Step 6 A ditto containing the lyrics is sent home with each child, and parents are asked to help their children practice the song.

Step 7 On subsequent music days, children continue to practice the lyrics both as a group and individually. For individual work, the teacher asks the child to sing and sign the song alone before the group. At first, children can look at the lyrics on the chart, but eventually they are expected to sing and sign from memory. The teacher helps and corrects the child until she can perform independently. He can post a chart on which he puts stars as the children master their songs. One music day per week is spent on introducing and mastering new songs. The second is spent on reviewing songs the children choose from a chart that lists songs learned in the past.

These procedures establish a repertoire of songs from which the teacher can choose before the children perform at assemblies and other community programs.

The following steps are used to teach children dances.

Step 1 The teacher (or teachers) demonstrates the entire dance for the children with accompanying record or musical instrument, if available.

Step 2 The teacher(s) demonstrate the beginning portion of the dance steps.

Step 3 The children practice with the help of the teacher(s).

Step 4 Steps 2 and 3 are repeated with additional dance steps until the entire sequence has been practiced, first without and then with music.

Step 5 The entire dance is practiced slowly, without music, until the children are able to follow the sequence of the dance from memory.

Step 6 The entire dance is practiced with music. Some dance days are spent introducing a new dance. Others are spent practicing the current dance and reviewing past dances. From time to time, children are asked to demonstrate steps individually.

As with the songs, these procedures establish a repertoire of dances from which the teacher can choose before the children perform at assemblies and other community programs.

PART 5

Management of the Instructional Environment

Individualizing Instruction 9

Importance of Individualizing Instruction

Individualized instruction has two basic components: (1) the teacher presents learning steps at a rate dictated by the child's ability to master the material. In using a curriculum, which should be sequenced in a specific order, the teacher introduces a new step only after the child has mastered the previous one. (2) Curricula are modified to accommodate each child's strengths and weaknesses. The teacher's responsibility is to move the child through the learning steps as quickly as possible. This involves finding alternate strategies for a child who is having difficulty, or giving enrichment materials to a child who excels in mastering the basic curriculum. In addition, the instruction of a child may be varied on the following dimensions: (a) time of day; (b) duration of instruction; (c) mode(s) of communication used for input and output; (d) behavior management techniques employed; and (e) instructional grouping.

Individualized Instruction During Tutoring Sessions

A tutoring session is a planned period when the teacher works with only one child at a time. The classroom schedule should be arranged so that the teacher can tutor each child daily; such an arrangement is essential for two reasons. First, tutoring is the most highly individualized, concentrated instruction the child can receive during the day. Because the entire period is devoted to the child's individual needs, the teacher focuses on the learning steps that apply only to that child. Second, the tutoring session is a special time for the child because he has the opportunity to work alone with the teacher. Children look forward to this experience and will ask when their turn is coming. Their positive attitude toward learning results.

Individualized Instruction During Group Lessons

During a group lesson, the teacher works with more than one child at a time; groups may be small, with two or three children, or larger. Although group size may vary, the teacher can still individualize learning for each child by planning objectives based on each child's abilities. Individualization within a group may require the children to learn differing numbers of items to master; some children will accomplish more complex tasks than others in the group. For example, during one week a teacher might be having daily group lessons on recognition of twelve printed verbs. Based on ability, some children will be required to master all twelve verbs, and others less, by the end of the week.

In another example, during a group time children at various levels of language development may be asked to respond with a word, a phrase, a simple sentence or a connected discourse. Children may be given different activities to perform, according to their needs and abilities. One child may be asked to comment on the weather, another to sequence the days of the week, and another to say the name of the day and the date. Expectations for children during any group lesson can be individualized in these ways.

Daily Schedules

Tables 9.1, 9.2, and 9.3 are examples of daily schedules for preschool, kindergarten, and primary/intermediate levels, respectively. Each contains four essential components that should be included in every daily schedule.

1. *Individual tutoring sessions with the teacher.* The teacher should have a daily planned period when she works with each child individually.

TABLE 9.1

Preschool Daily Schedule

Year: Teacher:

                                               Assistant:

9:00—10:00	Children: Teacher: Assistant:	small motor activities at desks individual tutoring with each child individual small motor tasks with each child
10:00—10:15	Assistant:	supervises bathroom time
10:15—10:30	Teacher: Assistant:	supervises snack time Break
10:30—10:45	Teacher and Assistant:	Calendar and weather activities
10:45—11:00	Assistant: Teacher:	supervises recess for children Break
11:00—11:25	Teacher: Assistant:	auditory training tasks large motor tasks (Teacher and assistant alternate groups, approximately 10 minutes per group)
11:25—11:50	Teacher: Assistant: Both: Both:	reading } M, Th, F English and vocabulary } alternate drill } groups language experience—Tuesday experience chart—Wednesday
11:50—12:15	Teacher: Assistant:	individual tutoring with each child supervises free-play or art activities
12:15—12:30	Assistant:	supervises bathroom time
12:30—12:50		Lunch for children (assistant leaves)
12:50—1:00		Get ready for buses (preschool children go home)

TABLE 9.2
Kindergarten Daily Schedule

Year:		Teacher: Assistant:

9:00—10:15	Teacher: Assistant:	individual tutoring with each child supervises children's seatwork and works individually with each child
10:15—10:30	Teacher: Assistant:	conducts "Opening" (flag, weather, calendar, songs) Break
10:30—10:45	Teacher: Assistant:	individual tutoring large motor development curriculum for each child
10:45—11:00	Assistant: Teacher:	supervises recess for children Break
11:00—11:30	Teacher: Assistant:	auditory training group lessons individual math
11:30—12:00	Teacher: Assistant: Both: Both:	group English or vocabulary ⎱ M, T, F lesson group English and ⎰ alternate vocabulary drill ⎱ groups language experience—Wednesday experience chart—Thursday
12:00—12:30	Assistant: Teacher:	supervises children's lunch, manners, clean-up writes letters to each parent; writes positive image building sentences with children for one child per day
12:30—12:50	(Assistant leaves) Teacher: conducts various activities for group:	
12:50—1:00	Get ready for buses (Kindergarten children go home)	

For the 12:30—12:50 row, activities by day:

Monday	Tuesday	Wednesday	Thursday	Friday
Developmental motor patterns and rhythms	Music and Listening bar	Library	P.E. (gym)	Sequence activities

TABLE 9.3
Primary/Intermediate Daily Schedule

Year:	Teacher: Assistant:

9:00—9:15	Teacher and Assistant: conduct opening activity
9:15—9:55	Teacher: individual tutoring with each child Assistant: individual math; supervises children's math worksheets at desks
9:55—10:20	Teacher: individual tutoring Assistant: group spelling and penmanship
10:20—10:40	Teacher and Assistant: Break Children: Recess
10:40—11:20	Teacher: group English lesson ⎱ alternate groups Assistant: group English drill ⎰
11:20—11:50	Teacher: reading groups Assistant: supervises children's reading worksheets at desks
11:50—12:10	Teacher: individual auditory training (special needs) Assistant: group auditory training
12:10—12:40	Lunch for children
12:40—1:10	Recess for children Lunch for teacher (assistant leaves)
1:10—1:45	Teacher: conducts various group lessons in science, social studies, career education, health ⎱ M, T, W, Th art—Friday
1:45—2:20	*Monday* music (songs) *Tuesday* gym *Wednesday* dance and rhythms *Thursday* library *Friday* literature
2:20—2:30	Get ready for buses (Primary and Intermediate children go home)

2. *Individual work with the assistant.* The teacher should plan daily periods of instruction when the assistant works with each child individually.

3. *Independent activities and seat work.* The teacher should plan learning tasks for children who are not working with the teacher or assistant during tutoring times. Each child does this work independently at his own desk or designated work area.

4. *Group work.* The teacher should plan daily group lessons, to be conducted by herself and/or her assistant.

Regardless of class level, all four components should be included in the daily schedule. Instructional materials and plans for each component become more complex as children move to higher grade levels.

The Tutoring Session

Possible components

Each child should receive at least 15 minutes of individual tutoring daily. The teacher should try to incorporate the following subjects into each tutoring session.

Speech and phonics. The three types of activities covered are imitation of consonant and vowel sounds in isolation, imitation of consonant and vowel sounds in words, and recognition of consonant and vowel sounds in print. For the two imitation tasks, the teacher says a vowel or consonant sound in isolation or in a word. Immediately following each sound production, the child attempts to imitate it as closely as possible. When the child masters a particular sound, she earns the privilege of putting a star on the appropriate chart in the tutoring area. For the print recognition task, the teacher shows a card with either a vowel or consonant sound on it. The child must read and correctly pronounce the sound. The criterion for mastery is independent accomplishment of the task on the first attempt that day. If the teacher corrects or cues the sound, the child can try again for mastery the next day. When mastery occurs, the child is allowed to put her star on the corresponding chart. In addition, correction of specific voice and fluency problems is undertaken during the tutoring period, with follow-through and continuous monitoring during the remainder of the school day and at home.

In upper grades or for children with advanced oral skills, instruction might include correction of articulatory errors in connected speech; refinement of the use of suprasegmental phonemes of stress, pitch, and juncture; and the dictionary use as an aid to correct pronunciation.

Vocabulary.   New vocabulary words in the current unit and review words from past units are covered. For young children, the teacher presents pictures or objects to the child in order to cue specific words. If the child misses a word, it is presented again the next day. The teacher reviews past vocabulary units systematically. When she has gone through all the units, she begins the process again. For older children, verbal cues such as questions and the use of synonyms, antonyms, or superordinate schema may be used to elicit responses.

Progress in mastering new sentence patterns is monitored in the daily tutoring session. Greg masters a new sentence pattern in total communication and is praised by his teacher.

Math.   Starting at preschool, counting and numeral recognition is practiced during tutoring. As the children advance, math instruction moves from the tutoring session to group instruction and independent seatwork.

Reading.   Each child reads two or three pages in the reading program, using total communication. The teacher introduces new words, corrects any reading errors, and asks comprehension questions about the story.

English sentence patterns.   English sentence patterns (from the English syntax curriculum described in detail in Chapter 6) are introduced, practiced, and reviewed. A sentence pattern chart is posted in the tutoring area; each time a child masters a sentence pattern, he puts a sticker on the chart. The criterion for mastery is independent accomplishment of the task on the first attempt on any given day, and the teacher writes the date of mastery next to each sticker on the chart. The teacher and children refer to the chart to determine the current day's sentence pattern. The teacher also systematically reviews one sentence pattern every day.

All five subjects should be taught daily. However, on occasion, a particular subject may not fit into the tutoring session because of

Greg gets to put a sticker on the chart next to the corresponding sentence pattern.

The teacher now writes the date the sentence pattern was mastered on the chart.

time considerations. In this case, the particular subject must be taught at a different time during the day.

A number of charts have been referred to in our discussion of the tutoring session. These records are essential to the accuracy of the teaching done during this time. Samples of the specific charts and a description of how to use them will be found in Chapter 10, entitled "Data Collecting Systems".

Working With Others to Facilitate Instruction

Classroom assistants

The assistant should be involved primarily in teaching children in small groups or individually. He will be assigned teaching tasks for which he has been specifically trained, while the teacher takes more complex ones. Examples of appropriate teaching areas to assign to the assistant are drill activities, vocabulary practice and review, math facts, printed word recognition, numeral recognition and sequencing, printing and writing exercises, spelling practice, art lessons, instruction for large and small motor-skill development, and supervising the use of some commercially prepared, programmed curricula. In contrast, the teacher is responsible for the more complex areas, such as auditory training, speech instruction, tutoring, reading, and English development.

The assistant also supervises non-instructional routines such as recess, bathroom time (for young children), and lunch. He occasionally prepares teaching materials, although this task should not interfere with his teaching duties. All instructional plans are prepared and explained in advance by the teacher. Directions to the assistant should be precise and specific. The teacher also prepares those data charts the assistant uses to record the children's daily progress in each area. It is the teacher's responsibility to monitor all activities of the

Pre-reading activities are an integral part of the preschool curriculum. Cheri is working on pre-reading skills with the classroom assistant.

assistant, to make instructional changes when necessary, and to use data gathered by the assistant to plan daily lessons.

Volunteers

A variety of people might be interested in volunteering time in the classroom. Potential volunteers are older children in the school (fifth or sixth graders), high school and college students, special education bus drivers from outside the district who may have time before their next run, and other interested people who have heard of the volunteer program. Although parents and relatives of children in the class may be invaluable assistants, caution must be used in determining whether their emotional involvement with their child and other hearing-impaired children creates undesirable tensions within the classroom.

The role of parents as volunteers in a classroom should never be confused by either the staff or the parent with the parent's participation in a parent education program. All volunteers, including parents, are in the classroom to contribute to the education of the children, in whatever way the staff determines best. The emotional or educational benefits to the volunteer are secondary to the needs of the children and staff. Parents in a parent education program may be included in the classroom, but their goal is to learn how to deal more effectively with their child at home. Therefore, their program focuses primarily on their needs rather than the needs of the class for additional assistance.

Volunteers should be used according to their abilities. Those who work with children skillfully, and can use total communication, may be used for simple teaching tasks with individuals or small groups. Those with other skills can be used for preparing materials.

Like directions given to assistants, directions to volunteers should be precise and specific. Generally, volunteers do not have the training to decipher general directions. The teacher must explain all steps in any activity. For instance, while the volunteer can record children's daily progress on data charts made by the teacher, the teacher bears the primary responsibility to make instructional decisions based on the collected data.

Data Collecting Systems 10

Monitoring Learning Through Data

The skillful teacher records data every day to monitor progress in the classroom and uses these data to plan learning steps for each student. The most efficient learning takes place in small steps that are sequenced precisely. They must be followed carefully; mastery on one is the criterion for moving to the next. Each child must be allowed to proceed at his own pace in mastering curricula. Data collection is necessary to the teacher who monitors a variety of curriculum areas. She must know exactly which step each child is working on during any instructional time so that she can teach children sequentially, allowing each his own pace. Without records the teacher cannot remember such a large amount of information. By using data, she avoids presenting the wrong learning step, teaching a curriculum out of sequence, or distorting the child's mastery progress by allowing him to remain on a learning step too long or moving him ahead before he is ready.

Methods used for keeping data

Charts used with children. Fourteen different types of charts will be presented in Tables 10.1 through 10.14; their uses are explained in the following text.

Tables 10.1 and 10.2 are the first two charts used in conjunction with the English Syntax Curriculum described in Chapter 6. Tech-

TABLE 10.1
English Sentence Patterns*

English Sentence Patterns	Child 1	Child 2	Child 3	Child 4	Child 5	Child 6
What is this ?						
Is this a/an (noun)? Yes, this is a/an (noun).						
What is that?						
Is that a/an (noun)? Yes, that is a/an (noun).						
What do you have?						
Do you have the (noun)? Yes, I have the (noun).						
What do you see?						
Do you see the (noun)? Yes, I have the (noun).						

*Note. As the child masters a sentence pattern he may place a sticker or a star on the chart in the appropriate space.

TABLE 10.2
English Sentence Patterns*

English Sentence Patterns	Child 1	Child 2	Child 3	Child 4	Child 5	Child 6
What is this? (use adj.)						
Is this a/an (adj.) (noun)? Yes, this is a/an (adj.) (noun).						
What is that? (use adj.)						
Is that a/an (adj.) (noun)? Yes, that is a/an (adj.) (noun).						
What do you have? (use adj.)						
Do you have the (adj.) (noun)? Yes, I have the (adj.) (noun).						
What do you see? (use adj.)						
Do you see the (adj.) (noun)? Yes, I see the (adj.) (noun).						

*Note. As the child masters a sentence pattern he may place a sticker or star on the chart in the appropriate space.

niques for teaching these sentence patterns and using the charts, as well as the complete sequence of sentences (questions and answers), was included.

Charts like Tables 10.3 and 10.4 can be drawn on the blackboard or posted in another conspicuous location to record each child's entirely correct, spontaneous English sentences. If the child needs any help in constructing the sentence, it is not recorded on the chart. To have a sentence written on the chart, the child must initiate a sentence to teacher or peer and must say it correctly the first time. The teacher and child then walk to the chart, the teacher prints the sentence in the child's column and they read the sentence together. At preschool level, the teacher reads and the child follows along. At older levels, the children read the sentences themselves. Reading is always followed by praise.

If a spontaneous sentence is incorrect, the teacher builds it into a correct one with the child, using the Again Technique (see Chapter 4, page 46). Thus, children learn that their attempts at complete sentences are expected and praised; this results in their continual attempts at communicating in sentences.

Table 10.3 is an example of typical preschool data, over a 2-month period. During her first year in preschool, the child usually needs several months of sentence building with the Again Technique before she says her first complete sentence spontaneously. Table 10.3 contains typical sentences being said by spring. Children 1, 2, and 3 are in their second year of preschool. That they have had almost two years of the Again Technique is reflected in their sentences which are more complex than those of children 4, 5, and 6 who are first-year preschoolers.

Table 10.4 is an example of a typical week's data in a kindergarten primary class, where children who have been taught with the Again Technique since preschool say sentences more frequently. Children 1, 2, and 3 are in primary class and children 4, 5, and 6 are in kindergarten. All children except child 6 have practiced sentences with the Again Technique since preschool. Child 6 entered kindergarten with no previous schooling; that he has had the Again Technique for only one month is reflected in his simpler sentences.

Charts like those presented in Tables 10.3 and 10.4 can be used with any child, regardless of hearing loss. Most of the children whose data are included in those charts have moderately severe to profound losses. All showed continual growth in ability to produce correct English sentences when the teacher used the chart in conjunction with the Again Technique.

TABLE 10.3
Spontaneous, Correct English Sentences
Preschool Sample

Child 1	Child 2	Child 3	Child 4	Child 5	Child 6
1. I want to wash.	1. I have a new shirt.	1. Where did you get that?	1. (Child's name) is not playing.	1. I am first.	1. (Child's name) is there.
2. Where is (child's name)?	2. What is that?	2. I did it three times.	2. Your name is ____.	2. Stand up.	2. (Child's name) is sick.
3. My mama is here.	3. I ate my cracker.	3. Where do you want me to put this?	3. (Child's name) is sick.	3. I am finished.	3. I have a sweater.
4. Where is (teacher's name)?	4. Is this your lunch?	4. I am not touching the floor.	4. (Child's name) is sleeping.	4. I want water please.	4. I am first.
5. (Child's name) and (child's name) are here.	5. This is your cake.	5. (Teacher's name), I can jump 10 times.	5. (Child's name) is first.	5. Yesterday was Monday.	5. (Child's name) is bad.
6. I want one kleenex.	6. I can do it.	6. I will open the door tomorrow.	6. I want to play with the box.	6. I am fast.	6. (Child's name) is first.
7. (Teacher's name) is funny.	7. What is your name?	7. Where did you get that?	7. Stop it.	7. I am cold.	7. I want to talk to (child's name).

TABLE 10.3 (cont.)
Spontaneous, Correct English Sentences
Preschool Sample

Child 1	Child 2	Child 3	Child 4	Child 5	Child 6
8. Where is my coat?	8. What are they?	8. I do not need it now.	8. Where is (child's name)?	8. What is that?	
9. (Teacher's name) is here now.	9. Daddy is working.	9. I do not like my sandwich because it has cheese in it.			
	10. What is this?	10. I saw her car.			
	11. I finished my book.	11. We both are 5 years old.			
	12. I am first today.				
	13. May I hit the bell?				
	14. My daddy is coming today.				

TABLE 10.4

Spontaneous, Correct English Sentences
Kindergarten/Primary Sample

Child 1	Child 2	Child 3	Child 4	Child 5	Child 6
1. I see another one.	1. Will you write about me on the calendar?	1. I have a little bicycle.	1. There was a pin in the rug.	1. May I turn off the lights?	1. Now you can eat.
2. Are you going to the ocean? I am.	2. The children are listening to the mother reading.	2. (Teacher's name), you are sitting on my desk.	2. I have two coloring books.	2. I have a toothbrush.	2. What are you doing here?
3. I saw (child's name) walking over there.	3. My mother painted my sister's room yesterday.	3. My hat is dirty; Grandmother will wash it.	3. This one was from Christmas.	3. May I carry the rope?	3. I am second.
4. The door is locked, (child's name).	4. May I turn the lights on?	4. Yesterday (child's name) forgot the swimming suit.	4. Please unbutton my jacket.	4. (Child's name) is not here.	4. I'm cleaning up.
5. I saw your brother.	5. My grandmother will come home in August or September.	5. Where is (teacher's name) purse?	5. I saw a big bubble in my milk and it popped.	5. May I help (child's name)?	5. I don't have any.
6. I will go to sleep on the boat.	6. I went before.	6. I want a new yellow raincoat or a hat.	6. Today my daddy and mommy will come and watch me swim.	6. May I go get my coat?	6. She's sick.

TABLE 10.4 (cont.)
Spontaneous, Correct English Sentences
Kindergarten/Primary Sample

Child 1	Child 2	Child 3	Child 4	Child 5	Child 6
7. I saw (*child's name*) pull my hair.	7. May I see the flower growing?	7. Yesterday I picked flowers.	7. This is my mommy's brush.	7. I was wrong.	7. I cleaned up the floor.
8. My mommy will buy a new notebook.	8. I went to the beach yesterday.	8. My mommy cut my hair on Saturday.	8. Remember, I knew all these.	8. Wait for me.	8. My mom gave it to me.
9. (*Teacher's name*), I cannot find my flower.	9. The door is locked.	9. I cannot find it.	9. I know something about (*child's name*).	9. May I have some water?	9. And I am fourth.
	10. I can run fast like (*child's name*).	10. My hearing aid is not working.	10. Are you going to eat lunch with us?	10. I will get the lunch.	
		11. I dreamed about you.	11. I know how to open my milk.	11. It is too noisy.	
		12. Later I will go sleep in Grandma's house.	12. I will not go on a boat.	12. The girl is cutting the paper.	

Tables 10.5, 10.6, 10.7, and 10.8 are examples of speech and phonics charts. They are large wall charts found in the tutoring area. Tables 10.5 and 10.6 record imitation skills for vowels and consonants. For mastery, the child must imitate a sound correctly after the teacher says it. Tables 10.7 and 10.8 record the child's ability to recognize in print and then to pronounce vowel and consonant sounds. For mastery, the child must read the sound independently and produce it correctly. The tables show one possible example of a speech and phonics system. If a teacher prefers a different one, it can still be used within the same chart format. When a child masters a particular sound, she earns the privilege to put a star on the chart. The left column of stars under each child's name represents sounds the child already knows when entering the class, determined by baseline testing at the beginning of the school year. The teacher simply asks the child to either imitate or read each sound, and gives a star each time the child is correct without any help. The right column of stars under each child's name represents sounds the child mastered throughout the school year. It is helpful to date the chart as the child masters each skill.

A variety of vocabulary charts can also be used. Tables 10.9 and 10.10 are example verb and adjective charts, appropriate for any elementary level. They show only small samples of possible verbs and adjectives to be taught during these years. These types of charts can be used for other parts of speech as well, and are used in the same way as the speech and phonics charts. The column of stars on the left under each child's name represents words the child used to describe events or pictures when entering the class, determined by baseline testing at the beginning of the school year. The right column of stars represents words the child mastered throughout the school year.

Table 10.11 is an example of a math chart. A wide variety of math skills can be recorded in this format; the one shown contains beginning math facts. The method for recording mastery is the method already detailed for the speech and phonics and vocabulary charts.

Table 10.12 is used with a rhythms program that teaches a variety of rhythm patterns pictured on cards. Symbols on the cards represent beats and rests in varying combinations, produced by either clapping, tapping the foot, using the voice, or playing a musical instrument. As the child masters each rhythm pattern, he receives a star on the chart.

Starting at the kindergarten level, and appropriate at succeeding levels, each child has an independent work chart taped to his desk. This chart is illustrated in tables 10.13 and 10.14. To use his chart, the

The daily schedule includes a time for each child to work individually with the classroom assistant. Johnny is identifying printed numeral words in this reading and math drill.

child must be able to read three things: the time, the day, and the specific activity. The time for using this chart remains constant, so the child can use it before he learns to tell time, a skill developing at kindergarten level. Upon entering kindergarten, the children learn to read the days of the week on their charts, as well as on the calendar. At this time, they will need help reading the days on their independent charts. They can develop this skill very quickly, usually within a month, if they practice daily. The third skill, reading the specific activity, takes longer to master. Children may need help throughout the first half of the initial kindergarten year. They are taught to read the activity on the chart and do the activity at the same time. By spring, most children can read the charts and accomplish activities independently. Concurrently, the teacher is working with individual children.

Records for teacher use. The teacher keeps a data book where he formally records all formative and summative data for each child. This data book serves as the basis for teacher accountability, instructional

TABLE 10.5
Vowel Sound Imitation

Speech Imitation	Child 1	Child 2	Child 3	Child 4	Child 5	Child 6
ēe	★	★	★		★	★
ōo	★	★	★	★	★	★
aw	★	★	★	★	★	★
ou	★	★	★	★	★	★
o-e	★	★	★	★	★	
i-e	★				★	★
a-e	★				★	★
u-e	★	★	★	★	★	
-u-	★	★	★	★	★	★
-a-	★	★	★	★	★	★
-e-	★	★	★	★	★	★
-i-	★		★	★	★	★
-o-	★	★	★	★	★	★
ŏŏ	★		★		★	★
oi	★	★	★		★	★

163

TABLE 10.6
Consonant Sound Imitation

Speech Imitation	Child 1		Child 2		Child 3		Child 4		Child 5		Child 6	
p	★		★		★		★		★			★
b	★		★		★		★		★		★	
m	★		★		★		★		★		★	
wh	★			★	★		★		★			
w	★		★		★		★		★		★	
f	★		★		★		★		★			★
v	★		★		★		★		★			
th	★			★	★		★		★			★
TH	★			★	★		★		★			
h	★		★		★		★		★			★
l	★				★		★		★			
r	★			★	★		★		★			
y	★				★		★					
t	★		★		★		★			★		
d	★		★		★		★			★		

n	k	g	ng	ch	j	sh	zh	s	z	x (ks)	q (kw)
★				★							
★	★	★	★	★	★					★	
★	★	★	★	★	★	★	★	★	★	★	★
★											
				★							
	★	★	★	★	★	★		★		★	★

165

TABLE 10.7
Vowel Sound Recognition in Print

Print Recognition	Child 1	Child 2	Child 3	Child 4	Child 5	Child 6
ēe	★	★	★	★	★	★
ōo	★	★	★	★	★	★
aw	★	★	★	★		★
ou		★	★	★		★
o-e	★	★	★	★	★	★
i-e	★	★	★	★	★	★
a-e	★	★	★	★	★	★
u-e	★	★	★		★	★
-u-		★	★			★
-a-	★	★	★			★
-e-			★			★
-i-	★	★				★
-o-	★					★
ŏo			★			★
oi	★	★	★			★

166

TABLE 10.8
Consonant Sound Recognition in Print

Print Recognition	Child 1	Child 2	Child 3	Child 4	Child 5	Child 6
p	★	★	★	★	★	★
b	★	★	★	★	★	★
m	★	★	★	★	★	★
wh	★	★	★	★	★	★
w	★	★	★	★	★	★
f	★	★	★	★	★	★
v	★	★	★	★	★	
th	★	★	★		★	
TH	★	★	★			
h	★		★			
l	★		★		★	
r	★		★	★	★	
y	★		★		★	
t	★			★	★	
d	★	★		★	★	

167

TABLE 10.8 (cont.)
Consonant Sound Recognition in Print

Print Recognition	Child 1	Child 2	Child 3	Child 4	Child 5	Child 6
n	★	★		★	★	
k	★		★	★	★	
g	★			★		
ng						
ch	★				★	
j	★			★	★	
sh					★	
zh						
s	★			★	★	
z	★			★		
x (ks)						
q (kw)						

Table 10.9
Verbs

Verbs	Child 1	Child 2	Child 3	Child 4	Child 5	Child 6
swim	★	★	★	★	★	★
walk	★	★	★	★	★	★
cry	★	★	★	★	★	★
drink	★	★	★	★	★	★
eat	★	★	★	★	★	★
jump	★	★	★	★	★	★
fall	★	★	★	★	★	★
sit	★	★	★	★	★	★
sleep	★	★	★		★	★
skate	★	★	★			★
sweep	★	★				★
run	★	★	★		★	★
blow	★	★				★
brush	★	★	★		★	★
climb	★	★	★		★	★
fly	★	★	★			
hide	★	★	★		★	★
kick	★	★	★			★

TABLE 10.9 (cont.)
Verbs

Verbs	Child 1	Child 2	Child 3	Child 4	Child 5	Child 6
pull	★	★				★
push	★	★				★
ride	★	★			★	★
throw	★	★		★	★	★
wash	★	★		★	★	★
write	★	★		★	★	★
break	★	★		★	★	★
carry	★	★				★
cough	★	★				★
crawl	★	★				★
cut	★	★		★	★	★
dance		★		★	★	★
drop		★		★		★
fight		★		★	★	★
sew		★				★
sneeze		★				★
tear	★	★				
yawn	★	★				★

TABLE 10.10
Adjectives

Adjectives	Child 1	Child 2	Child 3	Child 4	Child 5	Child 6
good	★	★	★		★	★
bad	★	★	★	★	★	★
long	★	★	★	★	★	★
short	★	★	★	★	★	★
early		★	★	★	★	★
late		★	★	★	★	★
afraid		★		★		★
brave		★		★		★
angry	★	★	★	★	★	★
happy	★	★	★	★	★	★
sad	★	★	★	★	★	
dark				★		★
light				★		★
high	★	★	★	★	★	★
low	★	★	★	★	★	★

TABLE 10.10 (cont.)
Adjectives

Adjectives	Child 1	Child 2	Child 3	Child 4	Child 5	Child 6
soft	★	★	★	★	★	★
hard	★	★	★	★	★	★
careful		★	★	★		★
careless		★		★		★
sharp			★	★		
dull				★	★	★
asleep	★	★	★	★	★	★
awake	★	★	★	★	★	★
first	★	★	★	★	★	★
last	★	★	★	★	★	★
tall	★	★	★	★	★	★
funny	★	★	★	★	★	★
right	★	★	★	★	★	★
wrong	★	★	★	★	★	★

TABLE 10.11
Math Facts
Sums to 5

Addition Math Facts	Child 1	Child 2	Child 3	Child 4	Child 5	Child 6
1 + 0 =	★		★	★	★	
1 + 1 =	★	★	★		★	★
1 + 2 =	★	★	★		★	★
1 + 3 =	★	★	★		★	★
2 + 0 =	★	★	★	★	★	
2 + 1 =	★		★		★	★
2 + 2 =	★		★		★	★
2 + 3 =	★		★		★	★
3 + 0 =	★	★	★	★	★	
3 + 1 =	★		★		★	★
3 + 2 =	★		★		★	★
4 + 0 =	★		★	★	★	
4 + 1 =	★		★		★	
5 + 0 =	★		★	★	★	

TABLE 10.12
Perceptual Motor

Perceptual Motor Cards	Child 1	Child 2	Child 3	Child 4	Child 5	Child 6
Card 1	★	★	★	★	★	★
Card 2	★	★	★	★	★	★
Card 3	★	★	★	★	★	
Card 4	★	★	★	★		
Card 5	★	★	★	★	★	
Card 6	★	★		★		
Card 7	★	★	★	★	★	
Card 8			★	★	★	
Card 9			★	★	★	
Card 10			★	★	★	
Card 11			★	★		
Card 12		★		★	★	
Card 13				★	★	
Card 14				★		
Card 15				★	★	

174

Card 16			★				
Card 17			★				
Card 18			★				
Card 19			★				
Card 20			★				
Card 21			★				
Card 22			★				

175

TABLE 10.13
Independent Work Chart, Beginning Kindergarten

Child 1	10:30 to 11:00 A.M.
Monday	Sequence Cards
Tuesday	Puzzles
Wednesday	Work with Ms. W.*
Thursday	Number Sequencing
Friday	Painting

Table 10.14
Independent Work Chart, Beginning Primary

Child 2	10:30 to 11:00 A.M.
Monday	Mirror Fingerspelling
Tuesday	Alphabet Sequencing
Wednesday	Painting
Thursday	Work with Ms. W.*
Friday	Printing Words on Chalkboard

*Note. Ms. W. is the assistant in the classroom.

decision making, progress reports, and I.E.P. summaries. The main records used only by the teacher to monitor children's communication skills development are shown in Tables 10.15 through 10.24.

Table 10.15 shows those skills the teacher monitors for each unit of vocabulary words. There are five skill areas the teacher monitors for each word; he records whether the child can 1) say, 2) sign, 3) read in print, 4) lipread, and 5) auditorally discriminate every word. Spaces are given for recording each skill performed by two children. Normally, all columns would be filled. The first three skills (say, sign, and read in print) are recorded as the child accomplishes them. Since mastery is expected in these areas, the teacher must monitor progress daily so that he knows which skills to teach. The last two skills (lipreading and auditory discrimination) are tested at the end of each unit. To check lipreading, the teacher presents each word in a unit by using the sentence, "Touch _____ ," where "touch" is signed and said and the vocabulary word is spoken with only minimal voice. To check auditory discrimination, the teacher presents each word in a unit, again using the sentence, "Touch _____ ," where "touch" is signed and said, and the vocabulary word is spoken in a normal voice. This time, however, the teacher's mouth is covered. Mastery is not required on these last two skills, because a hearing impairment can limit ability in lipreading and auditory discrimination. These abilities can be improved considerably, however, with continual exposure and practice.

TABLE 10.15
Sample Vocabulary Unit

Classroom Vocabulary (2 Week Unit)	Child 1					Child 2					Child 3					Child 4					Child 5					Child 6				
	*say	*sign	*print	*L.R.	*A.D.	*say	*sign	*print	*L.R.	*A.D.	*say	*sign	*print	*L.R.	*A.D.	*say	*sign	*print	*L.R.	*A.D.	*say	*sign	*print	*L.R.	*A.D.	*say	*sign	*print	*L.R.	*A.D.
table																														
chair																														
desk																														
pencil																														
paper																														
crayon																														
book																														
flag																														
chalk																														
chalkboard																														
eraser																														
scissors																														
paste																														
blocks																														
lights																														
mirror																														
glasses																														
hearing aid																														
wastepaper basket																														
ruler																														

Note. * Say—(child says word with understandable speech)
    * Sign—(child signs word correctly as he says it)
    * Print—(child recognizes word in print; expectations for mastery are varied according to child's abilities)
    * L.R.—(child can lipread word when teacher uses quiet voice without signing)
   *A.D.—(child can auditorally discriminate word seeing no visual cue)

Table 10.16 records a sample of each child's entirely correct, spontaneous English sentences over an entire school year. It is kept with the permanent academic records that are passed from teacher to teacher. As previously explained, the children's current, correct, spontaneous sentences are written on a chart for teacher and child use. Each week, the teacher transcribes at least one onto the permanent record form, shown in Table 10.16.

Table 10.17 records incorrect, spontaneous attempts at English. It is used in the same way as Table 10.16. Each week, the teacher writes at least one incorrect sentence on the permanent record form. They are not written on the blackboard and children are not shown them, because confusion could result from reading incorrect English.

Table 10.18 is used with the auditory training program. It is an example of the Household Sound Unit, one of several units in the program. Each sound to be auditorally discriminated is listed on the side of the chart. The three listening conditions—no background noise, music in the background, and voices in the background—are listed across the top of the chart. The teacher records household sounds as they are mastered under each listening condition by dating the appropriate box.

Table 10.19 is used with the large motor curriculum and shows the skills to be demonstrated by the 6-year-olds. As each skill is mastered, the teacher dates the appropriate box.

Tables 10.20 and 10.21 are used during individual tutoring time. Each child receives 15 minutes of daily, one-to-one instruction with the teacher, who makes two kinds of notations on the chart as she works with the child. On the current day's square, she stars any tasks the child accomplishes successfully. After each task has been attempted, she marks the step to be presented the next day. The tables show the charts after Monday's tutoring session. Activities for both a preschool (Table 10.20) and a primary (Table 10.21) classroom are presented. Monday's tasks were written the previous Friday. The tasks for the next day, Tuesday, were prepared during Monday's session.

Table 10.22 is used by the classroom assistant during a specified time period. Each child receives 10 to 15 minutes of daily, one-to-one instruction with the assistant. The table shows Monday's activities. The teacher specifies the task to be taught or tested in the top portion of each child's square, and the assistant describes the child's performance in the bottom portion of the square. The teacher uses each day's results to plan activities for the next day.

TABLE 10.16
Correct Spontaneous English Sentences

Child's Name _____	Year: _____ Teacher: _____
September	
October	
November	
December	
January	
February	
March	
April	
May	
June	

TABLE 10.17
Incorrect Spontaneous English Attempts

	Year: _____
Child's Name _____	Teacher: _____

September
October
November
December
January
February
March
April
May
June

TABLE 10.18

Auditory Training

Household Sounds (2 Week Unit)	Child 1			Child 2			Child 3			Child 4			Child 5			Child 6		
	Discrim. with no backgr. noise *	Discrim. with music *	Discrim. with voices *	Discrim. with no backgr. noise *	Discrim. with music *	Discrim. with voices *	Discrim. with no backgr. noise *	Discrim. with music *	Discrim. with voices *	Discrim. with no backgr. noise *	Discrim. with music *	Discrim. with voices *	Discrim. with no backgr. noise *	Discrim. with music *	Discrim. with voices *	Discrim. with no backgr. noise *	Discrim. with music *	Discrim. with voices *
door-bell																		
door slam																		
telephone																		
toilet flush																		
door knock																		

Note. * Auditory discrimination with no background noise
* Auditory discrimination with music in background
* Auditory discrimination with voices in background

Table 10.23 is used at the beginning and the end of the school year to monitor each child's growth in academic and nonacademic areas. Particular areas are detailed in the table. The same measures are used in the beginning and at end of the year for comparison purposes. Following the testing, the teacher and support staff go over the summaries to discuss children's growth. If there are concerns or special needs, they are discussed at that time, and an action plan is formulated.

Table 10.24 is an example of a fall progress report at kindergarten/ primary level. In this form, each academic area is detailed in order to specify a child's achievements to parents and future teachers. This format can be adapted for all elementary levels from preschool through intermediate grades.

Lopaka is being praised for his good sentence.

The classroom assistant keeps data on her individual work with the children in order to give the teacher feedback on each child's progress.

TABLE 10.19

Large Motor Skills
6-year level

Child's Name: Birthdate:	Teacher: Class:	
Skills:		Date Skill Mastered
Stands: On each foot alternately, eyes closed - right foot		
- left foot		
Jumps: Down from 12″, landing on toes maintaining balance		
Standing high (8 inches)		
Standing broad (2-3 feet)		
Jumps over rope (8 inches high)		
Running broad (3 feet)		
Jump Rope: Jumps rope, with child turning it himself		
Balance Beam: Walks full length, with alternating steps,		
unsupported (center raised section)		
Ball: Throws hand-size ball underhand 6 feet		
Throws hand-size ball overhand 6 feet		
Throws hand-size ball underhand at target 6 feet		
Throws hand-size ball overhand at target 6 feet		
Right-left: Walks on wooden slats (marked "right" and		
"left") in natural, alternating right-left pattern		
Follows wooden slats (marked "right" and "left")		
in varying patterns (optional)		
Comments:		

TABLE 10.20
Daily Individual Tutoring—Preschool Sample *

Day	Child 1	Child 2	Child 3	Child 4	Child 5	Child 6
Monday	Vocabulary Unit: Vegetables Review Unit: Fall Vowel: ee Consonant: b Counting: 0-9 Numeral Recognition: 0-9	Vocabulary Unit: Vegetables Review Unit: Toys Vowel: oo Consonant: m Counting: 0-3 Numeral Recognition: 0-3	Vocabulary Unit: Vegetables Review Unit: Toys Vowel: oo Consonant: f Counting: 0-5 Numeral Recognition: 0-5	Vocabulary Unit: Vegetables Review Unit: Animals Vowel: i-e Consonant: k Counting: 0-17 Numeral Recognition: 0-17	Vocabulary Unit: Vegetables Review Unit: Fall Vowel: aw Consonant: th Counting: 0-10 Numeral Recognition: 0-10	Vocabulary Unit: Vegetables Review Unit: Animals Vowel: o-e Consonant: d Counting: 0-15 Numeral Recognition: 0-15
Tuesday	Vocabulary Unit: Vegetables Review Unit: Toys Vowel: oo Consonant: b Counting: 0-10 Numeral Recognition: 0-10	Vocabulary Unit: Vegetables Review Unit: Fall Vowel: oo Consonant: f Counting: 0-4 Numeral Recognition: 0-4	Vocabulary Unit: Vegetables Review Unit: Fall Vowel: aw Consonant: f Counting: 0-5 Numeral Recognition: 0-5	Vocabulary Unit: Vegetables Review Unit: Toys Vowel: u-e Consonant: g Counting: 0-17 Numeral Recognition: 0-17	Vocabulary Unit: Vegetables Review Unit: Animals Vowel: aw Consonant: d Counting: 0-11 Numeral Recognition: 0-11	Vocabulary Unit: Vegetables Review Unit: Toys Vowel: i-e Consonant: j Counting: 0-16 Numeral Recognition: 0-16
Wednesday						
Thursday						
Friday						

*Note. The teacher determines the current day's step from the charts posted in the tutoring area and her daily tutoring book.

184

TABLE 10.21
Daily Individual Tutoring—Primary Sample*

Day	Child 1	Child 2	Child 3	Child 4	Child 5	Child 6
Monday	Vowel: oi Consonant: r Sentence Pattern Reading: Pages 9-12	Vowel: a-e Consonant: d Sentence Pattern Reading: Pages 25-26	Vowels: Review all 15 Consonant: v Sentence Pattern Reading: Pages 78-82	Vowel: -i- Consonant: s Sentence Pattern Reading: Pages 78-82	Vowel: -a- Consonant: q Sentence Pattern Reading: Book 19, pages 10-12	Vowels: Review all 15 Consonant: zh Sentence Pattern Reading: Pages 100-105
Tuesday	Vowel: -e- Consonant: r Sentence Pattern Reading: Pages 12-15	Vowel: a-e Consonant: t Sentence Pattern Reading: Workbook for pp. 25-26	Vowel: u-e Consonant: j Sentence Pattern Reading: Book 2 Pages 6-8	Vowels Review: all 15 Consonant: 2 Sentence Pattern Reading: Pages 82-85	Vowels: Review all 15 Consonant: x Sentence Pattern Reading: Auditory Discrimination of page 11	Consonants Review all 27 sounds Sentence Pattern Reading: Compre- hension questions on pages 100-105
Wednesday						
Thursday						
Friday						

*Note. The teacher determines the current day's step from the charts posted in the tutoring area and his daily tutoring book.

185

TABLE 10.22
Records Kept for Daily Individual Instruction with Assistant

Day	Child 1	Child 2	Child 3	Child 4	Child 5	Child 6
Monday	Spelling Test on verb unit .... Missed 2/15; breaking & dropping	Spelling Test on verb unit .... Excellent: All Correct	Test recognition in print of words on p. 36 - Reading Book .... Recognized only 2/5: and and run	Test Math Facts (sums to 10) .... Still gets confused when "O" is an addend	Work on proper formation of letters in first and last name (cursive) First name correct k, p, r formed incorrectly in last name	Practice sequencing capital letters of alphabet. .... MNOPQ not sequenced properly
Tuesday						
Wednesday						
Thursday						
Friday						

TABLE 10.23
Beginning and End of Year Summary

Child's Name:	B.D.:	School:	Teacher:	Class:	Year:	Date:

AUDITORY FUNCTIONING
  Degree of Loss:
  Adjustment to Hearing Aid:
  Progress in Auditory Training:

SPEECH AND PHONICS
  Imitation of Sounds in Isolation: Vowels—
                                    Consonants—
  Printed Recognition of Speech Sounds: Vowels—
                                        Consonants—
  Production of Sounds within Words:
  Connected Speech:
  Voice Quality:

LANGUAGE
  Vocabulary Words: Receptive—
                    Expressive—
  Sentence Patterns: Receptive—
                     Expressive—
  Spontaneous English: Correct Sentences—
                       Incorrect Sentences—
  Language Sample: Structured—
                   Non-structured—

ACADEMIC (Subjects appropriate to each grade level are tested)

MOTOR
  Gross:
  Fine:
  Perceptual:

SOCIAL/EMOTIONAL

SPECIAL CONCERNS, NEEDS OR RECOMMENDATIONS

Table 10.24
Progress Report

188

| NAME: | TEACHER: | GRADE: | DATE: | Days Present _____ |
| | | | | Days Absent _____ |

VOCABULARY

Can appropriately say and sign all words on the attached vocabulary word page except those that are circled.

READING

a. Can recognize in print all words which are starred on the attached vocabulary word page.
b. Has satisfactorily completed _____ in the _____ Reading Program.

LIPREADING

Can identify _____ of the Vocabulary words by pointing to the object, picture, or printed word when said by teacher with a quiet voice, using NO signs.

SPONTANEOUS

Spontaneous, grammatically correct English sentences are usually _____ words or more in length.
Examples: 1.
2.
3.

SPEECH and PHONICS

1. Vowels

a. Can imitate the following circled vowel sounds: ēe ōo aw ou o-e a-e i-e u-e -u- -a-
-e- -i- -o- ōo oi

b. Can recognize the following circled vowel sounds in print: ee oo aw ou o-e a-e i-e u-e
-u- -a- -e- -i- -o- ōo oi

2. Consonants

a. Can imitate the following circled consonant sounds: p b m wh w f v th TH t d
n h y l r k g ch j sh s z ng x (ks) q (kw)

b. Can recognize the following circled consonant sounds in print: p b m wh w f v th TH
t d n h y l r k g ch j sh s z ng x (ks) q (kw)

3. Alphabet Letters

a. small letters — Can recognize and name all small alphabet letters except:

b. capital letters — Can recognize and name all small capital alphabet letters except:

c. manual letters — Can recognize and name all manual alphabet letters except:

NUMBER CONCEPTS

1. Number Symbols

a. Can rote count _____.   b. Can recognize, name and sign numerals _____.
c. Can correctly write numerals _____ from memory.
d. Can sequence numerals _____ from memory.

2. Math Program — Has successfully completed _____ pages in the _____ Math Program.

Table 10.24 (cont.)
Progress Report

VOCABULARY WORDS (FALL 1977)

Classroom
desk
table
chair
pencil
crayon
hearing-aid
glasses
book
flag
chalk
chalkboard
scissors
paper
paste
blocks
mirror
light
wastepaper basket
eraser
pin
stapler
pen
thumb tack
ruler
tape
rubber band
pencil sharpener

2. **Adjectives**
happy
sad
confused
brave
afraid
friendly
hungry
sleepy
surprised
sick
hurt
angry

3. **Halloween**
Halloween
ghost
owl
pumpkin
jack-o-lantern
trick-or-treat
broom
moon
black cat
bat
mask
skeleton
spider's web
witch

4. **Verbs**
swim
walk
cry
drink
eat
jump
fall
sit
sleep
skate
sweep
run
blow
brush
climb
fly
hide
kick
pull
push
ride
throw
wash
write
break
carry
cough
crawl
cut
dance
drop
fight
sew
sneeze
tear
yawn

5. **Place Setting**
dishes
plate
fork
knife
spoon
bowl
cup
saucer
glass
napkin
placemat
tablecloth

TABLE 10.24 (cont.)
Progress Report

ENGLISH SENTENCE PATTERNS	When asked the appropriate stimulus question, _____ can consistently answer the following sentence patterns which are starred:	
This is a (noun).	I have (noun)(s).	No, the (boys, girls, etc.) are not (verbing) the (noun).
Yes, this is a (noun).	I see (noun)(s).	No, this is not a (noun).
That is a (noun).	My name is _____.	No, that is not a (noun).
Yes, that is a (noun).	I am a _____ (girl, boy).	No, the boy (girl, etc.) is not (verbing).
I have the (noun).	I am _____ years old.	
Yes, I have the (noun).	I am _____ (fine, OK, happy).	No, the girl (boy etc.) is not (verbing) the (noun).
I see the (noun).	I am _____ (1st, 2nd, etc.).	No, the boys (girls, etc.) are not (verbing).
Yes, I see the (noun).	I saw a (noun).	
This is a/an (adj.) (noun).	I will see a (noun).	No, a (noun) cannot (verb).
Yes, this is a/an (adj.) (noun).	I had a (noun).	No, a (noun) cannot (verb) a (noun).
I have the (adj.) (noun).	I _____ will have a _____ (noun).	No, I do not have the (noun).
Yes, I have the (adj.) (noun).	Yes, the (boys, girls, etc.) are (verbing) the (noun).	No, I do not see the (noun).
I see the (adj.) (noun).	Yes, the girl (boy etc.) is (verbing).	No, this is not a/an (adj.) (noun).
Yes, I see the (adj.) (noun).		No, this is not a/an (adj.) (noun).
The girl (boy) is (verbing).	Yes, the boy (girl, etc.) is (verbing) the (noun).	No, I do not have the (adj.) (noun).
That is a/an (adj.) (noun).	Yes, a (noun) can (verb).	No, I do not see the (adj.) (noun).
Yes, that is a/an (adj.) (noun).	Yes, a (noun) can (verb) a (noun).	
The boys (girls, etc.) are (verbing).		
The boy (girl, etc.) is (verbing) the (noun).		
These are (noun)(s).		
Those are (noun)(s).		

TABLE 10.24 (cont.)
Progress Report

DEVELOPMENTAL AND READINESS		

1. Large (gross) Motor Skills
2. Small (fine) Motor Skills
	a. skillful adequate needs more time to develop
	b. Needs more work in:
	
	a. can color
	b. can cut
	c. can trace forms, letters, numbers
	d. can copy forms, letters, numbers
	e. can print letters from memory
	f. can print numbers from memory
	g. can print spelling words from memory
	h. can print name from memory
	   first name
	   last name
		skillfully adequately with difficulty

AUDITORY TRAINING PROGRAM (with amplifi-cation)	1. Can identify and discriminate the following recorded transportation sounds:
	   rowboat ship's whistle car and horn helicopter airplane large truck train
	2. Can identify and discriminate the following recorded people sounds:
	   walking running clapping finger snapping humming whistling singing crying
	   coughing sneezing snoring
	3. Can discriminate and say 15 vowel sounds and 27 of the consonant sounds with back turned to speaker's voice
	4. Can sequence up to _____ vowel sounds and _____ consonant sounds in various patterns with back turned to speaker's voice
	5. Can identify and discriminate _____ of the vocabulary words with back turned to speaker's voice	

COMMENTS		

191

Classroom Management in Teaching 11

Planning individualized programs for language learning is based on the assumption that there is a classroom where all participants—teacher, aide. volunteers, and children—work harmoniously in a disciplined, efficient manner. To the extent that one or more participants in the learning process do not bear their share of responsibility for maintaining order and control, the learning of all the children will be impeded. This chapter briefly discusses typical ways in which a teacher can maintain classroom control while facilitating the children's academic and social growth. The word "discipline" is used throughout, but we use it in its classic sense of meaning "training intended to produce a specific character or pattern of behavior" and "controlled behavior resulting from such training." *(American Heritage Dictionary of the English Language, s.v. "discipline.")* Discipline is not synonymous with punishment.

Benefits to the Children and the Teacher

Training and reinforcement of socially acceptable behaviors are essential to the social development, vocational potential, and academic growth of hearing-impaired children. Since a hearing loss reduces the child's capacity to acquire socially acceptable behaviors through incidental learning, teachers and parents must consciously teach these skills even more than they would teach them to normally hearing children.

In the classroom, disciplined behavior positively influences the child's learning, social interaction, and self-image. For hearing-impaired children, every minute in school must count since there is so much to learn and so little time to learn it. Any student's poor behavior patterns, such as inattention, tantrums, silliness, and interference with other children, hinder the learning process for all children and thus are undesirable.

A teacher who maintains a disciplined classroom creates a calm, orderly atmosphere where each child and adult has the right and the responsibility to fulfill his or her assigned role in the learning process. Everyone *must* respect each other's roles. Students respect the teacher because he is consistent in his reactions to their behavior; students will be motivated to learn because academic accomplishment is praised and valued. They will develop good self-images and can carry their social skills and learning abilities into different situations.

Principles of Classroom Discipline

From the preschool years through high school, discipline is essential to an atmosphere for maximum learning. As children mature, they should be encouraged to take more responsibility for maintaining an orderly, pleasant learning environment. Even the youngest children in school are ready to assume some responsibility for controlling their behavior. We propose the following general guidelines to establish a disciplined classroom.

1. Positive reinforcement is the most effective discipline tool the teacher has. Positive reinforcement involves the immediate recognition and rewarding of an appropriate behavior by some overt means that pleases the child, such as praise, stars, checkmarks, smiles, tokens, clapping, handshakes, or hugs. Positive reinforcement is one of the most difficult techniques for many teachers to use. It is difficult to remember to attend to and praise the child who is sitting correctly when his neighbor is fighting. Yet praise is the best way to ensure that the child will continue to sit properly and that his neighbor will stop fighting. Positive reinforcement may come from the teacher, an assistant, a volunteer, or the child's peers. To be maximally effective, verbal praise should specifically address the child's behavior. For example, sentences like "I like the way you are sitting," or "You really listened carefully," or "You got more right today than yesterday, good work," are much better than generic praise such as "Good girl" or "O.K." They tell the child exactly what it was that she did well and that the teacher would like it repeated.

2. The teacher's ultimate responsibility is to decide on rules for behavior and convey them to other classroom members.   Children must be socialized—taught the skills and rules of proper conduct—just as they must be taught the skills and rules of arithmetic, spelling, and science. Adults bear the responsibility of teaching the advantages of acceptable behavior and the disadvantages of unacceptable behavior. The younger a child is, the firmer the guidance to acceptable behavior patterns must be. As children mature, they should be seriously consulted on classroom rules; acceptable standards of conduct should be formulated by the teacher and students together. In the end however, the teacher, by virtue of authority, knowledge, and legal accountability, must take responsibility for making and enforcing the best decisions.

3. Bad behavior habits seldom, if ever, go away by themselves. The longer a child is allowed to use inappropriate behaviors, the harder it is to extinguish them and substitute appropriate behavior patterns. When inappropriate behaviors interfere with classroom learning or persist for a long period, particular disciplinary procedures must be used. (See page 197.)

4. Firmness, consistency, and follow-through.   A firm teacher directs children convincingly. This is not to say that the teacher must act inflexibly, ignore the child's input, or lack empathy. Rather, once she makes a decision, she lets the children know she means it.

A consistent teacher is predictable. He establishes expectations on which the children can depend. The children in his class are familiar with his way of handling specific situations. They know that certain behaviors are acceptable in the classroom and others are not. Again, this is not to say that classroom rules are inflexible or unchanging. Rethinking and reorganizing rules is fine as long as the children are kept informed.

A teacher who follows through monitors her system of rules. Once the rules have been established, the teacher must respect them if she expects the child to. If a teacher chooses to ignore rules sporadically, she will encourage the children to do the same. At times, following through seems like a lot of work; the temptation is to ignore a child breaking a rule. By doing this, however, the teacher actually creates

195

more work for herself in two ways. First, the next time she wants to discipline that child, she will have to work even harder to convince him she means what she says. If the child disobeyed the first time and got away with it, he will persist even longer the second time, expecting to get his way again. Second, a teacher who does not follow through encourages the child to test her, looking for the next time she will ignore her own rules.

Firmness, consistency, and follow-through comprise a disciplinary formula effectively used with normal children—that is, those without special behavioral problems. A teacher who uses the formula well is rewarded with a calm classroom atmosphere. Mild warnings and penalties stop misbehavior after the teacher has established her credibility

Typical example: disciplinary formula

During a group English language lesson, the children have been instructed to watch the teacher. Yet one child persists to hit and tease her neighbor.

What to do. To apply the guidelines, the teacher uses a previously determined warning. The teacher says, "Stop playing and watch, or you will leave the group and stand over there _____ ." He then indicates the predetermined place (behind a screen or near a wall). If the child complies and resumes attending, the teacher reinforces her behavior by saying, "Good, now you are watching." If the child continues non-compliance, the teacher must follow through by enforcing the warning. Either the child is told to stand up and go to the predetermined place or is physically assisted to comply when the teacher walks her to the place stated. This follow through is essential to establishing credibility, freeing the children from the necessity for testing the teacher. Once a teacher establishes this credibility she can usually stop misbehaviors by using positive reinforcement or a warning.

Typical example: positive reinforcement for responding to present request

The teacher has asked a child to read a sentence, signing and saying each word. She reminds him to say his s sound correctly where it occurs. The child reads the sentence correctly, taking care to pronounce the s sounds.

What to do. In this situation, the teacher might praise the child just for reading each word correctly. She might say, "Good, you read that sentence very well." However, she must remember that she also requested good speech. So she should praise the child for pronouncing *s* sounds correctly with a comment like, "Good speech! You said all your *s*'s beautifully." The teacher must remember what she has asked and praise the child for it immediately.

Typical example: positive reinforcement for responding to past request

During a group science lesson, child 1 has to be continually reminded to watch each child take turns answering questions. Positive feedback is given each time child 1 complies. These reminders are necessary for several days. The next day, the teacher notices child 1 independently watching child 2, who is answering a question.

What to do.   The teacher immediately praises child 1. He says, "Wonderful, you remembered to watch." Child 1 is pleased her teacher noticed that she remembered. This technique requires that the teacher have a good memory because he must always be looking for children accomplishing past requests.

Special Disciplinary Procedures for Children with Behavior Problems

Setting up a behavior program

Any child who does not respond to the measures previously described is a candidate for a special behavior program. Such a program involves five steps.

1. Pinpoint the behaviors to be changed.   The teacher must specify which behaviors he is trying to change. He must be able to describe them in an objective, countable way because he will document an increase or decrease in the behaviors. Behaviors can be grouped in pairs; an undesired one to be decreased is paired with a desired one to be increased. The program should be designed so that an increase in the acceptable behavior ensures a decrease in the unacceptable one.

2. Plan consequences for the behavior.   An acceptable behavior should be followed immediately by something valuable to the child as a reward. Likewise, an unacceptable behavior should be followed immediately by a penalty. A skilled teacher remembers that rewards and penalties should be child-oriented. Something that seems rewarding to the teacher may disinterest the child. While the teacher may think that candy is rewarding, the child may not like sweets. Likewise, what appears to be a penalty to the teacher may actually be desired by the child. The teacher may think of scolding as punishment but the child may actually welcome it because she craves any form of attention. The appropriateness of rewards and penalties can be judged only by monitoring the child's reactions to them.

3. Keep data on the behavior.   The teacher should prepare a form for recording data. Weekly sheets with a separate section for each day can be used. Usually, frequency of behavior is tallied; that is, each time a behavior occurs it is marked on the data sheet so that a daily total can be taken. In this way, daily increases and decreases in behavior can be monitored. Several days of baseline data should be recorded before the program is started. The frequencies of the appropriate and inappropriate behaviors during baseline should be tallied as a basis for comparison with later behaviors after consequences—rewards and penalties—are started.

4. Evaluate the data.   Data determine action; they tell the teacher what to do next. If desirable behaviors are increasing or undesirable ones decreasing, then the program is working. If frequency of behaviors is constant when it should be changing, the program is not working. If desirable behaviors are decreasing or undesirable ones increasing, the program is not working.

A skillful teacher lets the data talk to her. If the data indicate that the techniques are working, then she should continue the behavior program as is. If the data show that the techniques are ineffective, then she must find one or more components to change. Consequences for behaviors should be examined first. A new reward or a new penalty could be used. The teacher can also check the behaviors pinpointed for change. They may need to be defined more specifically. Vague definitions limit the teacher's ability to count data accurately, as well as confuse the child's expectations of how to act for a reward. If the teacher decides that the definitions in the behavior program are specific enough after evaluating them, then she knows that a consequence, either positive or negative, must be changed.

Only one consequence (either one reward or one penalty) should be changed at a time. This rule must never be broken. If a change in a consequence is followed by a change in the behavior data, the teacher can reasonably conclude that the former has caused the latter, assuming that other aspects of classroom routine have remained the same. If a change in more than one consequence is followed by a change in the data, the teacher has no way of telling which new consequence influenced the child's behavior. To restate: only one consequence—reward or penalty—should be altered at a time, and each change should be monitored independently through the behavior data in order to judge its effect.

5. Phase out the behavior program. The teacher's goal is to help the child develop good behavior that will eventually be independent of a special program. After the teacher's daily monitoring of data (including any necessary changes in rewards and penalties) has shown that there is the desired behavior change, the teacher will want to phase out his behavior program and help the child use self-control to maintain appropriate behavior. Commonly, phasing out is accomplished by either lengthening the time between rewards or decreasing the frequency of rewards while maintaining social approval. At first, the penalty for the unacceptable behavior is also maintained. Later, the penalty can be phased out after the child has demonstrated good self-control.

Typical example

A teacher has a child with a special behavior problem in her classroom. Whenever she makes a request of him, whether it is routine, such as hanging up his coat, or academic, such as imitating a speech sound, the child shakes his head no and does not comply. The teacher has tried a variety of normal disciplinary procedures and none have been effective.

What to do. The teacher sets up a special behavior program for this child by following the five steps outlined previously.

1. Pinpoint the behavior to be changed. The undesirable behavior is the child's shaking his head no and refusing to comply. This behavior is to be counted and decreased. The teacher will tally it each time it occurs. The incompatible, competing behavior is compliance. Each time the teacher directs the child and he complies, rather than shaking his head, the teacher will tally this also.

2. Plan consequences for the behavior. Since the teacher has noticed that this child looks to his peers for approval, she will use peer attention as part of both the reward and the penalty. Peer approval can be incorporated into the reward for good behavior. If the child complies the first time asked, the teacher will give him a big hug and children and teacher will clap for him. The first time the child shakes his head no after any request, the teacher will give him a warning by repeating the request and telling him that if he doesn't comply he will have to leave the room (therefore removing him from his peers). For example, she might say to a child who said "no" to a request to read, "Read this sentence or you will sit outside the door." If he then complies, she praises him; If he does not, she takes his chair and has him sit just outside the classroom door.

3. *Keep data on the behavior.* The teacher will design a weekly chart to monitor pinpointed behavior. It might look like this:

	M	T	W	Th	F
No's	total	total	total	total	total
Compliance	total	total	total	total	total

After her chart is ready, she takes 2 or 3 days of baseline data. In other words, before she starts rewards and penalities she records the frequency of complying and saying no. These behaviors will be compared to the child's behavior after she begins her program. When she starts the behavior program she is prepared to follow through with the consequences she has planned. Each time the child shakes his head no, she makes a hatch mark in the *no* section of the appropriate day. Likewise, each time the child complies, she puts a hatch mark in the *compliance* section of the appropriate day. The data is recorded after she responds to the child with the predetermined penalty or reward. At the end of the day, the hatch marks in each section are totaled.

4. *Evaluate the data.* Suppose the data chart looks like this:

	M	T	W	Th	F
No's	total 12	total 15	total 14	total 4	total 2
Compliance	total 6	total 5	total 5	total 15	total 16

During the 3 baseline days (Monday, Tuesday, and Wednesday), the child said "no" 12, 15, and 14 times and he complied only 6, 5, and 5 times. On Thursday and Friday, after rewards and penalties were started, he said "no" 4 and 2 times and complied 15 and 16 times. Desirable behaviors have increased and undesirable ones have decreased, so the program is working. The teacher will continue it as is.

Suppose the chart looks like this:

	M	T	W	Th	F
No's	total 12	total 15	total 14	total 9	total 11
Compliance	total 6	total 5	total 5	total 8	total 7

On this chart, the baseline data (Monday, Tuesday, and Wednesday) are the same as those on the previous chart. On Thursday and Friday, after rewards and penalties were started, the saying no has decreased slightly to 9 and 11 times and complying has increased slightly to 8 and 7 times. Although this may be the beginning of a positive trend there is not enough data yet to judge. A few more days of data must be taken to find out:

	M	T	W	Th	F
No's	total 9	total 12	total 12	total	total
Compliance	total 8	total 5	total 6	total	total

Now there is enough data to show that the frequency of the behaviors has not changed markedly. On Monday, Tuesday, and Wednesday, the child was still saying no 9, 12, and 12 times and was still complying only 8, 5, and 5 times. The program is not having the desired effect, so the teacher must change one aspect. Perhaps the child does not like to be hugged; she might want to try only clapping as the reward, starting on Thursday of Week 2. Suppose she gets the following data:

	M	T	W	Th	F
No's	total 9	total 12	total 12	total 4	total 2
Compliance	total 8	total 5	total 6	total 15	total 16

On Thursday and Friday, the change she has made resulted in a decrease in no saying to 4 and 2 times and an increase in complying to 15 and 16 times. Now the behavior program is having the desired effects. The teacher will continue it as is.

Suppose the data chart looks like this:

	M	T	W	Th	F
No's	total 12	total 15	total 14	total 17	total 18
Compliance	total 6	total 5	total 5	total 1	total 1

Again during the baseline period, the child said "no" 12, 15, and 14 times and complied 6, 5, and 5 times. On Thursday and Friday, after the program was started, no saying increased to 17 and 18 times and complying decreased to 1 and 1 times. Undesirable behaviors are increasing and desirable ones are decreasing, so the program is not working. The teacher must find one aspect to change. Perhaps the child enjoys sitting outside the room because people are walking by and interacting with him. Therefore, the teacher may decide that he will sit behind a screen in the classroom, starting Monday of the next week. Now, suppose she gets the following data:

	M	T	W	Th	F
No's	total 4	total 2	total 2	total	total
Compliance	total 15	total 16	total 16	total	total

On Monday, Tuesday, and Wednesday, the change made has resulted in a decrease in no saying to 4, 2, and 2 times and an increase in complying to 15, 16, and 16 times. Now the teacher's behavior program is having the desired effects. She will continue it as is.

5. *Phase out the behavior program.*   Let's continue with the example where the teacher and the child's peers clap every time he complies and the child sits behind a screen in the classroom every time he says no. When data indicate the child's *no* behavior has stabilized to a predetermined low frequency, the teacher begins to phase out her behavior program. Perhaps she will consider the behavior stable if the child says no only two times per day over a 2-week period while compliance remains high. As this trend begins in her data, she will start planning her phasing-out program so that she can start it immediately after 2 weeks of acceptable behavior. During phasing out, the penalty will remain constant; the child will still sit behind the screen each time he says no.

There are several possible ways of phasing out rewards. As usual, the data is monitored to make sure the reward is working. Time between rewards can be increased or their frequency can be decreased. In this example, the child has been rewarded on a frequency basis; every time he has complied, his teacher and classmates have clapped. Therefore, the frequency of the reward needs to be decreased. The teacher might begin by clapping every other time the child complies. After a week, if her data remain constant, she can decrease the frequency of the reward again. This pattern can be followed until clapping has been phased out. If *no's* increase, she has made her phasing out change too soon and must repeat the previous step. Remember that teacher praise is never phased out. It is an essential skill to be used with all children.

Parent involvement

A child with behavior problems at school will probably have behavior problems at home too. Most likely, the parents of such a child will feel they need some help handling her. Once a successful behavior program is established at school, it can be extended to the home. Parents can learn to manage their child's behavior by using the techniques established by the teacher. In this way, the discipline program will be consistent between home and school, and parents will receive needed direction.

The teacher must monitor the home program carefully. Each morning the parent can send a note to the teacher, reporting daily progress at home. Notes from the parent may contain data on the child's behavior. The teacher then sends a reply to the parents each afternoon. The teacher evaluates the success of the home program each day. If it is going well, he should praise the parents and encourage them to continue. Whenever the teacher decides a change is necessary he should suggest it in his afternoon notes. Sometimes phone calls are necessary to make sure changes are understood, as well as to maintain good contact.

Typical example

Continuing our example from the section *Setting Up a Behavior Program,* say the teacher has established a successful behavior program for a child. When the child complies, the class and teacher clap for him. When the child says no, he must sit behind a screen in the classroom. Now the teacher wants to extend this program into the home because the parents have trouble controlling the child.

What to do.   The teacher phones the parents and asks them to come to school for a conference. The child is not present at this initial meeting. The teacher begins the discussion by presenting the child's behavior program at school, explaining it's every aspect and showing the parents her data to illustrate the program's success. After she completes her explanation and answers any questions, the teacher then tells the parents that she would like them to use the behavior program at home.

Next, the teacher invites the parents into the classroom to observe the techniques she is using with their child. If one or both parents arrange to come, she tells them she can continue the conference after the observation. At that time she and the parents can both decide specifically what the parents will do at home. If the parents cannot come to school, the teacher will use telephone conferences to decide on techniques for the home program. She outlines the following techniques of the home behavior program: if the child says no they should tell him to comply or he will have to sit in a designated penalty area of the house, facing away from the rest of the family. For example, he might have to sit in a corner of the family room, facing the wall. If the child complies, then all members of the family clap for him and praise him. The teacher gives the parents data sheets to be filled out daily. After the parents understand exactly what they are to do at home, they can begin immediately.

Because the teacher will need to monitor progress at home every day, she should ask the parents to send in the current week's data sheet every morning with their child and encourage them to write comments. The teacher will check it every day and send it back each afternoon with a reply. If the program is going well she praises the parents. If she does not see the expected changes, she will need to communicate further. Sometimes confusion can be cleared up within the daily notes; other times, a phone call or another conference is necessary to determine the problem.

When the data from home indicate the child's behavior has improved and stabilized, it is time to start phasing out the program. Perhaps, as in the classroom, teacher and parents will consider the behavior stable if the child says no at most two time per day over a 2-week period, while compliance remains high. The parents must learn the phasing-out program used at school. The teacher tells them to clap for their child every other time he complies rather than each time. They should continue phasing out by using the intervals that have worked at school. The teacher should explain that the penalty will remain constant. She continues monitoring the data sheets every day during this time, and if problems arise, she readjusts the phasing-out intervals. When the desired behavior remains stable after phasing

Leisure time reading can be used as a reward for good work in the classroom. John and Jim have earned this special privilege.

out is complete, the teacher tells the parents they can stop sending daily data sheets, but should contact her immediately if any change occurs. She also reminds the parents to continue praising good behavior and to use this skill whenever possible.

References

Abeson, A. Education for handicapped children in the least restrictive environment. In M. Kindred, J. Cohen, D. Penrod, & T. Shaffer (Eds.), *The mentally retarded citizen and the law.* New York: The Free Press, 1976.

Advisory Committee on Education of the Deaf. *A Report to the Secretary of Health, Education, and Welfare by his Advisory Committee on the Education of the Deaf.* Washington D.C.: U.S. Department of Health, ducation, and Welfare, 1964.

American Annals of the Deaf, April, 1978. (Directory issue)

Barry, K. *The Barry system: A system of objective language teaching.* Colorado Springs: Gowdy Printing and Engraving Co., 1914.

Birch, J., & Stuckles, E. *Relationship between early manual communication and later achievement of the deaf.* University of Pittsburgh Project No. 1969. Cooperative Research Branch of the United States Office of Education, March, 1963—February, 1964.

Bloom, L., & Lahey, M. *Language development and language disorders.* New York: John Wiley and Sons, 1978.

Buell, E. M. *Outline of language for deaf children, Book 1.* Washington, D.C.: The Volta Bureau, 1954.

Calvert, D. R. *An approach to the study of deaf speech.* Report of the proceedings of the International Congress on the Education of the Deaf. Washington, D.C.: U.S. Government Printing Office, 1964.

Carroll, J.B. *Language and thought.* Englewood Cliffs, N.J.: Prentice Hall, 1964.

Chiba, C., & Semmel, M. I. Due process and least restrictive alternative: New emphasis on parental participation. In M. I. Semmel & J. L. Heinmiller

(Eds.), *Viewpoints: The Education for All Handicapped Children Act (P.L. 94-142)—Issues and implications.* Bloomington: School of Education, Indiana University, 1977.

Cooper, R. L. The development of morphological habits in deaf children. In J. Rosenstein & W. MacGinitie (Eds.), *Research studies on the psycholoinguistic behavior of deaf children.* Washington, D.C.: The Council for Exceptional Children, National Education Association, 1965.

Diana v. State Board of Education, C-70-37 (RFP Disr. Ct. N. Cal. 1970)

Doctor, P. V. (Ed.), *Communication with the deaf: A guide for parents of deaf children.* Lancaster, Penn.: Intelligence Printing Co., 1963.

Eisenson, J., Auer, J., & Irwin, J. *The psychology of communication.* New York: Appleton Century Crofts, 1963.

Final Technical Report of the Institute on Applied Linguistics for the Hearing Impaired (Monograph). New York: Teachers College, 1966.

Fitzgerald, E. *Straight language for the deaf: A system of instruction for deaf children (3rd ed.).* Texas: The Steck Company, 1937.

Fusfeld, I. The academic program of schools for the deaf. *Volta Review,* 1955, *57,* 63—70.

Groht, M. A. *Natural language for deaf children.* Washington, D.C.: The Volta Bureau, 1958.

Hall, R. A., Jr. *Introductory linguistics.* Philadelphia: Chilton Company, 1964.

Harris, G. M. *Language for the preschool deaf child* (2nd ed.). New York: Grune and Stratton, 1950.

Hart, B. O. *A child-centered language program.* Report of the proceedings of the International Congress on the Education of the Deaf. Washington, D.C.: U.S. Government Printing Office, 1964.

Heider, F., & Heider, G. A comparison of sentence structure of deaf and hearing children. *Psychological Monographs,* 1940, *50.*

Hester, M. *Manual communication.* Report of the proceedings of the International Congress on the Education of the Deaf. Washington, D.C.: U.S. Government Printing Office, 1964.

Hirsch, I. *Communication for the deaf.* Report of the proceedings of the International Congress on the Education of the Deaf. Washington, D.C.: U.S. Government Printing Office, 1964.

Hockett, C. F. *A course in modern linguistics.* New York: Macmillan, 1958.

Huizing, H. Potential hearing in deaf children—Its early development and use for auditory communication. In A. W. G. Ewing (Ed.), *The modern educational treatment of deafness.* Washington, D.C.: The Volta Bureau, 1960.

Joyce, Z. No. 2035-60 (C.C.P. Allegheny County, Pa., 1975)

Jensema, C. The relationship between academic achievement and the demographic characteristics of hearing-impaired children and youth. Series R, Number 2. Washington, D.C.: Gallaudet College, Office of Demographic Studies, 1975.

Kirk, S. *Educating exceptional children.* Boston: Houghton Mifflin, 1962.

Lowenbraun, S. *An investigation of the syntactic competence of young deaf children.* Unpublished doctoral dissertation. Columbia University, 1969.

Lowenbraun, S., & Scroggs, C. The hearing impaired. In N. G. Haring (Ed.), *Behavior of exceptional children: An introduction to special education.* Columbus, Ohio: Charles E. Merrill, 1974.

Magner, M. E. *Language development in the lower school of the Clarke School for the Deaf.* Report of the proceedings of the International Congress on the Education of the Deaf. Washington, D.C.: U.S. Government Printing Office, 1964.

Miller, J. Practices in language instruction. *Exceptional Children,* 1964, *30,* 355—358.

Miller, W., & Ervin, S. The development of grammar in child language. *The acquisition of language: Monographs of the Society for Research in Child Development,* 1964, *29,* 9-34.

Mills v. Board of Education of the District of Columbia, 348 F. Supp. 866 (D.D.C., 1972).

Mycklebust, H. R. *The psychology of deafness.* New York: Grune and Stratton, 1960.

New York Association for Retarded Children v. Carey. 393 F. Supp. 715 (E.D. N.Y., 1975).

Pennsylvania Association for Retarded Children v. Commonwealth of Pennsylvania, 334 F. Supp. 1257 (E.D. PA., 1971).

Perier, O. *The role of parents in the education of deaf children.* Report of the proceedings of the International Congress on the Education of the Deaf. Washington, D.C.: U.S. Government Printing Office, 1964.

Pickles, A. M. Hearing aids in home training. In A. W. G. Ewing (Ed.), *Educational guidance and the deaf child.* Manchester, England: Manchester University Press, 1957.

Pintner, R., & Paterson, D. A measure of the language ability of deaf children. *Psychological Review,* 1916, *23,* 413-436.

The Council for Exceptional Children, *Professional Standards for Personnel in the Education of Exceptional Children.* Washington, D.C.: National Education Association, 1966.

Pugh, G. Summaries from appraisal of the silent reading abilities of acoustically handicapped children. *American Annals of the Deaf*, 1946, *91*, 331-349.

Reichstein, J., & Rosenstein, J. Differential diagnosis of auditory deficits. *Exceptional Children*, 1964, *31*.

Rosenstein, J., & Cooper, R. L. Language acquisition of deaf children. *Volta Review*, 1966, *65*, 73-82.

Scouten, H. L. *The place of the Rochester method in American education of the deaf*. Report of the proceedings of the International Congress on the Education of the Deaf. Washington, D.C.: U.S. Government Printing Office, 1964.

Simmons, A. E. A comparison of the type-token ratio of spoken and written language of deaf and hearing children. *Volta Review*, 1962, *64*, 417-421.

Soskin, R. M. The least restrictive alternative: In principle and in application. *Amicus*, 1977, *2*(6).

Stephanie L. No. J-184924 Juv. Div. (C.C.P. Phila. County, 1977).

Summary of Progress in hearing, language, and speech disorders. Research Profile No. 4. Washington, D.C.: U. S. Department of Health, Education, and Welfare, 1965.

Templin, M. C. *Certain language skills in children*. Minneapolis: University of Minnesota Press, 1930.

United States Department of Health, Education, and Welfare. Proposed rules for education of handicapped children: Implementation of part b of the Handicapped Act. *Federal Register*, August 23, 1977. (a)

United States Department of Health, Education, and Welfare. Proposed rules for non-discrimination on basis of handicap: Programs and activities receiving or benefiting from federal financial assistance. *Federal Register*, May 4, 1977. (b)

Watson, T. J. *The use of residual hearing in the education of deaf children*. Washington: The Volta Bureau, 1961.

Wyatt v. Stickney. 344 F. Supp. 387 (M.D. ALA., 1972).